# The Brand New
# BEAT THE BUMF!

For a complete list of Management Books 2000 titles,
visit our web-site on http://www.mb2000.com

# The Brand New
# BEAT THE BUMF!

*Kathryn Redway*

2000

First published in 2005 by Management Books 2000 Ltd
Forge House, Limes Road
Kemble, Cirencester
Gloucestershire, GL7 6AD, UK
Tel: 0044 (0) 1285 771441
Fax: 0044 (0) 1285 771055
E-mail: mb2000@btconnect.com
Web: www.mb2000.com

Printed and bound in Great Britain by Digital Books Logistics Ltd of Peterborough

British Library Cataloguing in Publication Data is available

ISBN 1-85252-472-3

# Contents

# Preface

Information and its evil twin brother 'bumf' are found on the airwaves, in boardrooms, in the classroom, in personal mail and in after-dinner speeches. New technology has spurred massive growth in the availability of information. This book aims to educate readers in how to meet these new challenges by adopting techniques that they never would have had the opportunity of picking up at school or college.

My initial thoughts on handling information were crystallised by Tony Buzan, to whom I am forever grateful. This book is intended to complement Tony's work, in particular the Brain Trust which he has founded. (Buzan Centres Ltd, 54 Parkstone Road, Poole, Dorset, BH15 2PG, UK).

In writing this book, I would like to thank all participants on my workshops who have contributed to updating my thinking. For permission to use, to varying extent, extracts from books or articles, I thank Professor Geoffrey Best, *The Financial Times* and Roger von Oech.

# Introduction

Throughout this book I use case studies to illustrate bumf victims. The people depicted in the case studies are information management novices, thoroughly ill-equipped to face the barrage of material that confronts them in their lives and jobs every day. The scenarios described in the case studies are inspired by the people who attend my information management workshops. We begin with a typical day for Barbara.

Barbara arrives at her office one morning, unpacks her briefcase and takes out a brown file, three magazines and half a dozen one page memos. She also has a report which needs editing. In her 'out-tray' Barbara places a journal and all the one-page memos. Everything else stays on her desk, joining yesterday's unfinished business in one large pile. She sighs as the post arrives on her desk: the stack is over an inch thick. Barbara logs on to her computer and finds she has a dozen email messages. Before retrieving them she glances at her diary and realises that she has only five minutes before she is due at an important meeting. She grabs her brown file as she hurries out of the door.

As she slides into the meeting, a director is discussing whether a supplier should be changed. Barbara struggles to remember the problem. Although she read the report late the night before, she can only remember the name of the murderer in the film that was competing for her attention. To make up for her lapse of memory, Barbara makes copious notes, not knowing what information was in the report or even which issues are really relevant.

When Barbara returns to her office she attempts to tackle her emails and post. But a constant stream of interruptions and visitors prevents her from getting to grips with it. A lot of the stuff in her in-tray requires information which is not readily available - she puts these things aside. As she works, telephone calls distract her attention.

As the day ends Barbara fills up her briefcase, knowing that she will look at only a fraction of the material during the course of the evening. The report which needs editing also goes in. Despite trying to tackle it a few times she has not started it yet; even the appearance of the report seems to deter her. Barbara reaches home feeling dissatisfied with her day, already knowing that tomorrow will not be much different.

Barbara is being overwhelmed by information. Everything that comes across her desk seems useful and empowering yet, when facing the stream of facts, Barbara is numb, unreceptive and unable to distinguish between valuable and unimportant information. She fails to return all her messages and many of her replies are past the deadlines required. Barbara is suffering from *infectious information*. She needs to prepare offensive and defensive strategies.

In preparing a defensive strategy Barbara needs to divide her material into **information** and **bumf**.

## What is the difference between information and bumf?

**Bumf** - the piles of paperwork, reading matter and information that have to be dealt with but are of little interest, and that hinder you from accomplishing your primary tasks.

Bumf comes from the phrase 'bum fodder', meaning toilet paper. As you stare at the volumes of paper that crowd your desk, this might be worth remembering to set you in the right mental mood for discarding less useful material.

For our purposes, the definition should be widened to include all the sources from which information is obtained. Bumf can obscure useful information in meetings, on the radio, in conversations, on the TV, as well as through all sorts of electronic media. All this information enters the brain and competes for attention, time and memory space as it is categorised, pigeon-holed, recalled and used at appropriate times.

Bumf may be likened to the snowstorm which obscures or hides the glimmer of light (information) towards which one is struggling. One of the aims of this book is to raise a fundamental issue:

**As an information receiver, how frequently is the information you receive 'instructive'?**

With a bit of practice you should find that extracting the useful from the bumf becomes an essential part of your routine and you will probably wonder how you ever coped before.

## *Beat the Bumf* and you

Managing your time and information load should mean managing this book as well. If you are snowed under like Barbara, then the last thing you need is a lot of extra reading.

This book is divided into two parts - 'Defence against Bumf' and 'Offence against Bumf'. It is not designed to be read from cover to cover.

● In Part 1, **'Defence against Bumf'**, you will find ways to regain control of ceaseless incoming information on paper, electronically, or in meetings. It will also give you tips to improve your memory and discourage interruptions.

● In Part 2 **'Offence against Bumf'**, you will find techniques to read faster and present documents that are easier to absorb.

The chapters are designed to be used as units. You can read straight through or skip from chapter to chapter. At the end of each chapter, start off on the technique that you have just learned using the hands-on exercises suggested to consolidate your reading.

Now, I am making a foolish assumption: you have some problems with information flow and you want an easier life. Do some of these general problems apply to you?

- You receive many documents and your e-mail is cluttered up with many types of information which will never be of interest to you.
- You receive information of little or no use to you.
- You spend too long in meetings or reading information.
- You have difficulty in assessing clearly the purpose for which you need the information contained in a particular document (or information source).
- Few meetings or documents are crucial or very important to you for the effective performance of your job.
- In a particular document the information you want is highly diluted by information you do not want.
- You feel guilty about the piles of manuals, periodicals and reports waiting to be read.
- You think other people manage their 'bumf' but you don't.
- You are unsure about what information to keep and how to file it.
- You have discovered that taking decisions, generally, is a painful process.

Specifically, in **handling bumf**, do you recognise any of the following difficulties? Have you ever:

|  | Go to Chapter |
|---|---|
| • felt that a document was uninviting and left it aside? | 6 |
| • re-read a word, a paragraph, a page for fear of missing something? | 6 |
| • had difficulty in finding your way around a document? | 8 |
| • found it difficult to make notes from a document? | 8 |
| • invested much time to absorb and retain information | 4 |
| • had difficulty in recalling information? | |
| • wondered which document to tackle first? | 2 |

- experienced poor concentration?    6
- felt you had to remember everything you read?    6
- wished you could extract 'important' information fast?    8
- found that you did not understand what you read?    8

With **meetings**, these are the most commonly cited problems.
   Have you ever:

                     Go to Chapter

- felt that you attended too many meetings?    2
- been to meetings which were badly chaired?    2
- had difficulty writing the agenda or the minutes?    2
- felt the topics discussed in meetings overlapped?    2
- wished meetings ended on time?    2

# Part 1

## Defence against Bumf

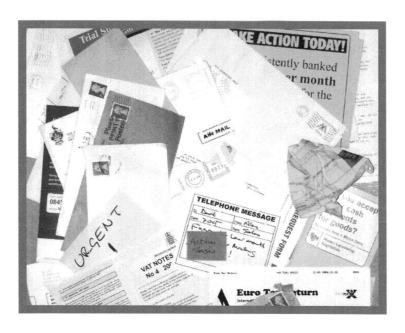

# 1

# Controlling Bumf and Your Reading

> **READING IS AN ATTITUDE**
>
> **VISUAL AND NON-VISUAL SKILLS**
>
> **READING AND UNDERSTANDING**
>
> **SO, WHAT DO WE CONCLUDE?**
>
> **READING AND GOALS**
>
> **THE POWER OF ANTICIPATION IN READING**
>
> **HANDS-ON EXERCISES**

## Reading is an attitude

Technology has freed us from many boring and tedious tasks. It has, however, resulted in a massive increase in the amount of information capable of changing hands. In a week, we come across more information than the average person in 19th century Europe received in a year.

Today, information is mass-produced, controlled and driven by your expectations. How many unsolicited offers or letters have you received this week? What information did your organisation or boss restrict? What information do you hear a great deal on English television that never appears on German television? How frequently do you hear without listening? See without perceiving? Read without understanding?

Handling this massive influx of bumf requires the right mental attitude. To face the problems head on you need:

☑ the **desire to improve**. You have to be prepared to increase your reading speed, your time management and your ability to identify essential information. Opening this book is an important first step.

☑ **confidence**. It is important to improve and believe that you can.

☑ **assertiveness**. You must accept that you do not need to know everything by recognising that some information is irrelevant while other bits of information are vital for you.

☑ the **ability to relax**. Once rid of anxiety, you will find it easier to use memory, organise information, rely on your current knowledge, and establish your reading objectives.

**To control bumf, be ...**
**motivated, confident, assertive, and relaxed**

## Visual and non-visual skills

When you read a phrase, your brain dissects it in a number of different ways. It is capable of recognising whole words and phrases in hundredths of a second without the need to consider each letter. To demonstrate this consider the following passage:

*Es war Anfang Mai und, nach nasskalten wochen, ein falscher Hochsommer eingefallen. Der Englische Garten, obgleich nur erst zart belaubt, war dumpfig wie im August und in der Nahe. Der Stadt voller Wagen und Spazierganger gewesen.*
(from *Der Tod in Venedig* by Thomas Mann)

If you are unable to speak German, the only way you can read it is by examining each word and guessing how it might be pronounced. As only one or two of the words have any obvious meaning, this is quite a slow process. You will find your eyes often need to examine each word a few times. Compare this to something in English where recognition can be used:

*A wonderful bird is the pelican,*
*His bill will hold more than his belican.*
*He can take in his beak*
*Food enough for a week,*
*But I'm damned if I see how the helican.*

(D. L. Merritt, 1879-1954)

The words in this limerick are familiar and some even evoke images so they are instantly recognised by the brain. You probably found that you had more difficulty with the last word in the last line and the last word in the second line. Your brain was unable to recognise the 'shape' of these words so it had to hover over them a little longer to examine each letter.

This process is the same for whole phrases. Try reading what you see below quite quickly.

**Paris**
**in the**
**the spring**

Unless you are a very slow and careful reader, you will have thought that the phrase said *'Paris in the spring'*. Look again and you will see that it actually says 'Paris in the the spring'. Your brain is adept at recognising whole phrases which are familiar in very small periods of time. This enables you to scan very quickly through documents looking for information, if you discipline your mind in the right way.

## Reading and understanding

It is also important to remember that your brain connects whole sentences to other sentences and can relate this to other information from the rest of your knowledge base. To illustrate this, consider the following:

*But silver bromide is so much less soluble than silver chloride that a far smaller concentration of potassium bromide will produce a precipitate, while silver iodide, the least soluble of the three, is precipitated in very low iodide concentrations. This method can be used to separate silver chloride from silver iodide. The usual explanation is that 'silver chloride is more soluble in ammonia than silver iodide' but this is not a satisfactory way of stating the facts.*

(from Theoretical and Inorganic Chemistry, Philbrick and Holmyard, p 190)

Unless you are well versed in the solubility of silver halides in ammonia solutions, the chances are that you cannot remember the information in the passage. If you do remember, it is unlikely that you will remember it half an hour from now. So your ability to retain information is very dependent upon your understanding of and familiarity with the subject matter.

To summarise, good understanding involves:

- being able to select and understand what you need
- connecting this new information to existing knowledge
- retaining and recalling that information

## So, what do we conclude?

When you read, your brain is involved in the following simultaneous steps.

☑ **Visual recognition of symbols -** words which are not familiar are read by examining each character.

☑ **Visual recognition of whole words or phrases -** whole-word recognition is facilitated by its position in a logical phrase.

☑ **Comprehension and the integration** into semantic or related knowledge - a process of evaluating the knowledge.

☑ **Memorising** the information.

☑ **Responding** to the information - what do you do with it?

Visual and non-visual skills can be improved. The simple task of improving visual skills is described in Chapter 7. We call it improving the dynamics of reading. It is easy.

Much more challenging are the non-visual components of reading: using imagery, increasing comprehension, and improving long-term retention of information. These are dealt with in Chapters 4, 6 and 8.

## Reading and goals - what are we looking for?

To obtain information quickly when reading, it is important to have a goal. You adopt different reading strategies depending upon the type of information you want to extract.

Imagine you are reading the time on a clock. If you wish to catch a train, the clock tells you how long you have to do this in comfort. The **goal of reading the clock** in this context is to calculate the time you have left to catch the train.

How did you read the menu last time you were in a restaurant? If you are vegetarian, you will have skipped the meat dishes. If you were on a budget you only considered dishes in your price range. The **goal of reading the menu** is a selective process in which large sections of the menu are discarded before a dish is chosen.

---

# M e n u

**Dinner is served between 6.30pm and 10.30pm.**

**Please find a table, note the number and order at the bar.**

### Hors d'Oeuvres

Mousse aux Courgettes 3.50
Velouté de Poivrons doux et
  Tomates 3.50
Provençal Hors d'Oeuvres 4.00
Cheese Soufflé 4.00

### Fish

Wild Salmon Cakes 9.00
Halibut in Beurre Blanc 9.50
Devilled Whitebait 8.00
Crab Salad 9.50

### Poultry

Pheasant with Puys Lentils 10.50
Timbale of Duck 9.00
Roast Chicken with Watercress
  Stuffing 8.50
Braised Quails 10.50

### Vegetarian

Avocado Pilaff 6.00
Watercress Salad with
  Mushrooms and Parmesan 5.50
Mushroom and Asparagus
  Rissotto 6.50
Fettuccine al Burro e Formaggio
  7.50

### Entrées

Agneau Epice with Couscous 10.50
Boeuf en Daube 10.50
Osso Bucco 12.50
Steak and Kidney Pudding 10.50

### Desserts

Lemon Sorbet 3.00
Cassatta alla Siciliana 3.00
Normandy Apple Tarte 3.50
Lemon Tarte 3.50
Espresso coffee 2.50

---

*Figure 1.2 - Menu*

If you are reading a map, you will probably want to know how to get to your destination and how long it will take you. The **goal of reading a map** is to find out which roads lead from one place to another and to plan your route.

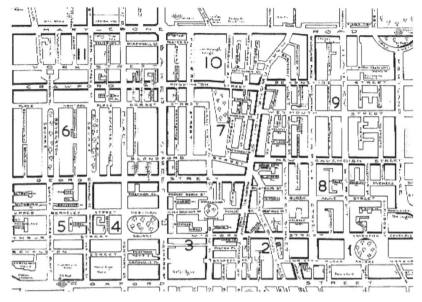

*Figure 1.3 - Map*

If you have a family member who is allergic to some food then you have to scan product labels to find the offending ingredient. In my family, I have to read food labels to see if the product contains monosodium glutamate. The **goal of reading the label** is to ascertain whether the product is 'safe'.

When opened consume at once

## *Spooner's Somerset Sauce*

The perfect compliment to alcoholic and
night-time beverages

By appointment to his late majesty
King George IV

'Never again will I touch a good malt whiskey
without lacing it with a few drops of SSS.'

General G.S. (Ret'd) of Cheltenham

'Every night I sleep like a log since I started
to make my Horlicks with SSS.'

Granny G. of Princeton

### Made to a unique secret recipe by
### S.Spooner and Company since 1793

INGREDIENTS:- MATURED BOMBAY DUCK. OLD MOLASSES,
DEHYDRATED EGGS, DRIED SNOEK, FRUCTOSE,
MONOSODIUM GLUTAMATE. EMULSIFIERS E471, E472,
E47S, COLOURS (LUTEIN, BETA-CAROTENE, RIBOFLAVIN).
LACTOALBUMEN, STABILISER (CARRAGEENAN).

*Figure 1.4 Bottle label*

These examples show that visual information is not enough to achieve
the goal of the reading exercise. We use different reading strategies
depending on the goal. You read telephone directories, newspapers,
and instructions to install a DVD-recorder in different ways. You read
with a purpose in mind which interacts with the information you are
reading and the knowledge you already have. If you neglect to think
about purpose or goals first, you are likely to choose the wrong
reading strategy.

# The power of anticipation in reading

Have you ever tried to read a complex legal document? Unless you are a lawyer you will probably find you have to read every word of a contract in order to understand it. Lack of familiarity with the subject and with the words used make it difficult for you to guess or anticipate what you are going to read.

Pick up a newspaper and select an article. Can you make sense of it by reading only half the printed words? Try to eliminate or abandon roughly five words per sentence. If you are familiar with the style and subject matter then you will find this task a lot easier.

Imagine that you are half-way through a thriller. The action takes place in a European city in the middle of summer. When you pick up the book again, will you be thinking 'The author hasn't mentioned penguins yet. I wonder if he'll describe the breeding condition of penguins on the shores of the Antarctic?' Probably not. Instead you may be anticipating likely thrilling events taking place in the summer in Europe.

Similarly, a sentence which begins, 'Management books are written around themes, reports contain specific information and minutes of meetings' is not likely to be followed by 'eat', 'elephant', 'trumpet' or 'rhododendron'. You can make a reasonable guess, amongst 100,000 alternatives. Possible words are selected because the context limits choice. Develop and use your power of anticipation. Have the confidence of previous experience, previous knowledge and familiarity with the context which will enable your mind to speed up your comprehension of the text.

Recent research has highlighted the importance of anticipation in processing language. Dr Rosaleen McCarthy, a neuro-psychologist lecturer at King's College, Cambridge explains, 'If you can anticipate what the next word in a sentence could be, you will not necessarily notice if some of the letters in that word are out of place' (quoted in *The Times*, Sept 23, 2003).

Test this with the fllowonig wdros in tihs snetnece; if you can siltl raed it wouthit porbelm, you are vlaidtnaig the rseacrh!

It seems that as long as the first and the last letters of the word are in the right place, it will always be understood, whatever the order the rest are in. Dr McCarthy continues, 'The human brain is a lot more tolerant than we had perhaps realised, and it has to cope with disrupting in every-day life.'

Already in 1919, Dr Bates, an American ophthalmologist, in *Better Eyesight Without Glasses* (10), wrote 'We see very largely with the mind, and only partly with the eyes.' To paraphrase his belief, it can be argued that we read largely with the mind and only partly with the eyes.

## Hands-on exercises

☞ Start a log of all non-work related reading material that you receive and make a note of its purpose. Review your log in a month and take appropriate action.

☞ Develop anticipation by reading one paragraph of a document upside-down.

☞ Develop anticipation by placing a card on a line so as to hide the bottom half of the words and read four or five lines in this way.

☞ Practise picking an article in a newspaper and deliberately reading only one word in three. Summarise the article. Are you missing much of importance?

# 2

# Controlling Bumf and Your Time

---

**DO YOU SUFFER FROM PILES?**

**DELEGATE**

**IMPROVE YOUR MANAGEMENT OF MEETINGS**

**DEAL WITH ELECTRONIC TEXT**

**HANDS-ON EXERCISES**

---

## Do you suffer from piles?

In the introduction, we met Barbara who, like most people, suffers from 'piles'. Which pile of untouched work deserves priority? Different demands on time require prioritising.

All work can be categorised as:

- urgent, must be attended to immediately
- should be completed within the next few days
- can be put aside (if other things are pressing) for a week or so
- need never do.

There is a fifth category - the sort of job where you can save a lot of time and stress by doing parts of it as you come across it in the course of current or urgent work. For example, suppose you have to give a presentation in four weeks' time. Rather than waiting for the job to move into the urgent category, you can gradually assemble the information required whenever you come across appropriate data. Collecting the data, unedited and unsorted in a file awaiting attention, saves much hassle in the days immediately before its delivery. Otherwise, as Murphy's Law forecasts, if you start looking for the information only at the last moment, it will not be available and a crisis will develop.

Defend yourself against the accumulation of bumf by dividing your workload into two piles.

- The first pile contains jobs which require immediate attention and action.

- The second pile contains documents which require some time to be read or which can only be dealt with after more information has been assembled.

## Delegate

Barbara could consider delegation as another weapon against dealing with bumf. She should try to identify the work, perhaps part of a task for which she is responsible, that could be done by somebody else and then delegate it.

Work can be delegated in three directions:

↑ It can be delegated **upwards** if your boss does not give you full authority to complete a task. It stands to reason that if you are unable to finish something without help from above then you can request help to do your work.

← Delegation **sideways** comes about by having colleagues who are better equipped to do a job than you are. This usually happens if they have specialist knowledge, control the resources or are not under the same time constraints as you.

⬇ Delegation **downwards** is the most obvious. Junior staff quite often appreciate this because it shows your trust in them or it enables them to develop skills that they might eventually market elsewhere.

# Improve your management of meetings

### Case Study

John is responsible for the European communications in a multi-national. With offices in each of the European countries, John's time is caught in a spiral of meetings, frequently overseas. He chairs some meetings, others he attends. John expresses frustration, even anger, and complains that his life has become engulfed in meetings. Specifically, he says, 'we have too many of them; often I am there and what is discussed does not concern me directly. Also, we have some senior colleagues who go on and on, digressing, loading the meeting with bumf and, as a result, meetings overrun. I don't seem to get anything done any more and time just disappears.'

### Minimise the frequency, maximise the efficiency

Like John, do you find that one of your most frequent bumf problem is associated with meetings? John, and perhaps you, needs to rebuild his defence against a culture that abuses the purpose of meetings.

First, could John suggest alternatives to meetings? For example, before he decides to hold a meeting or chair one, there are several questions to ask - firstly, is this meeting necessary? Are there other ways to take a decision or brief people?

● How about circulating widely a memo for people to approve or comment? Email makes this very efficient. There are two drawbacks though: the first is that one does not get the benefit of interaction, second, no one makes a synthesis of ideas.

- Could he take the decision himself, without involving everyone?

- What about phoning the people concerned and asking their opinion, or briefing them over the telephone?

- Conference calls or video links can save a lot of travelling time but can be quite difficult to chair if there are too many people.

- It is always worth attempting to amalgamate meetings. Could 'one hour, monthly' meetings replace '45 minutes, fortnightly'?

- If a meeting is essential to decision making, remember that with more than four people, coming to a conclusion becomes much more difficult

If John is asked to attend a meeting, there are other options.

- Rather than attending a meeting, he could express his interest, but decline to attend as he cannot see how he can actively contribute and ask for a copy of the minutes.

- He could consider the risks of not attending some meetings.

- He must develop the habit of saying 'No' if he cannot see how attending a meeting can contribute anything or be useful to him.

### Shorten the length of meetings

Frequently, short meetings are the most effective. If you are arranging a meeting, do you always take the following steps?

- ☑ Prepare a detailed **agenda**. For example, instead of 'Computer system installation schedule', write: 'Computer system installation is four weeks behind schedule and £60,000 overrun caused by supplier difficulties. The meeting is to consider how the installation can get back onto schedule and within budget, how supplier difficulties can be reduced and what action can be taken to minimise current problems'. List who is to contribute what.

☑ Estimate the **timetable** for decision(s) to be made during the meeting and list it on the agenda.

☑ Choose a **finishing time** that will create a sense of urgency, for example, just before lunch or, best of all, on a Friday afternoon.

☑ Put **less important items** at the front of the agenda to minimise latecomers' disorientation, with important items in the middle and a popular, easily agreed item last, to end the meeting on an up-beat note of achievement.

☑ Ensure that all attendees are properly **briefed** about difficult or complex subjects beforehand to eliminate time wastage in the meeting.

☑ **Intervene** firmly, but politely, when fellow participants attempt lengthy and rambling speeches. A good chairperson recognises the signals and tactics of such people and ensures that the meeting is kept moving.

☑ Suggest holding the meeting in someone else's office. It is easier to leave a colleague's office than your own.

Here is a checklist you can use as a reminder.

## Before the Meeting

1. Ensure that a programme or agenda is prepared. Outline the purpose of the meeting clearly. The agenda also states the beginning and finishing time, date, place and names of participants.

2. Notify all appropriate people to attend. Supply agenda and necessary briefing papers, allow time enough for them to be read in advance.

3.  Book a room for the meeting with appropriate facilities.

4.  Nominate a secretary or scribe, making sure he or she knows the relevant duties. If possible, have overhead projector (OHP) transparencies or flipcharts prepared beforehand.

5.  Check that all invitees can attend.

## During the Meeting

6.  Start on time, even if people are missing.

7.  The chairperson:
    - reiterates the purpose of the meeting
    - defines the facts and constraints of the situation
    - establishes the task(s) of the meeting.

8.  The chairperson guides people through the meeting. He or she ensures that the subject of the meeting is adhered to, formulates questions to act as a catalyst and develops group interest and involvement.

9.  All members should participate. If not, why?

10. The scribe keeps notes and uses an OHP or flipchart to display key concepts, suggestions, parameters, etc.

11. Recap on progress regularly, points of agreement and disagreement. Check understanding and acceptance.

12. Acknowledge all contributions, including those not used. Recognise degrees of feeling and changes of opinion.

13. Allow limited excursions from the subject if they appear to be opening up an important new line of thought which may affect the subject. Suggest, if appropriate, that these be made the subject of

action after the meeting and perhaps the subject of a subsequent meeting.

14. Delegate action items and unresolved issues to attendees for action outside the meeting, so that problems are answered without the need for another meeting, or ensure that proper preparation is made for the next meeting.

15. Obtain agreement on responsibility for action and deadlines.

16. Maintain a spirit of enthusiasm and good humour.

17. Finish firmly on time.

### After the meeting

18. Ensure that accurate minutes are issued and distributed to all attendees within two days, with decisions and future actions, by whom and when, clearly noted.

19. The minutes can be circulated to those persons who need to be informed of decisions made in the meeting, but did not attend.

# Deal with electronic text

It used to be only IT Departments which complained of information explosion - now everyone does. People feel that the volume of information they face threatens to engulf them. And the greatest gripe today is towards information generated electronically. Hoards of trigger-happy employees hit the 'send all' button without a care. There is still a feeling that emails are disposable and people pay little attention to what they put in an email. In fact, far from disposable, emails are one of the hardest form of IT communication to erase. An email replicates itself like bacteria. Once sent, it is almost impossible to ensure that no copies survive. At best, bumf replicates itself through other people's servers; at worst, some of these emails become the source of embarrassment as inaccurate rumours spread like a disease at the touch of a button. Keep in mind that email is a compromise as a communication medium since it replaces personal human interaction. So, do not abuse it. Now, let us look at Richard who suffers from some of these symptoms.

---

### Case Study

Richard is Head of Division in a multinational engineering company. He is in charge of a project that involve people in three European countries. 'I receive about eighty emails a day. Half of them are not addressed to me personally, about ten of them are spam and today I received an email from a colleague about four feet away from my desk. I cannot concentrate on anything for long because the incoming emails keep interrupting me. And when I go to a meeting and switch my voicemail on, I come back to an accumulation of emails and half a dozen recorded verbal messages. The combination of electronic, audio and print information has become too much. I feel overloaded.'

---

Richard has lost control of incoming information. What strategies are there to help him?

First there are techniques to ease reading on the screen. They do not differ radically from techniques for dealing with other types of bumf. It is therefore a little surprising that people expect a brand new technique to cope with electronic mail or other electronically driven documents! Richard could apply the same basic instructions that they use for paper to a screen.

## Twelve easy steps to reading a screen

📺 To read faster, use the scroll mechanism or the cursor (or caret) as a pacer or prompter.

- Make your peripheral vision work for you: push your chair another foot away from the screen. You will avoid eye strain and will be able to take in lines rather than individual words.

- Avoid printing out the message, even if it is two or three pages long. If you do, delete the electronic version.

- Use the techniques of scanning and skimming to pick up keywords to decide whether messages are worth reading thoroughly (see Chapter 7).

- Check your messages regularly - say a minimum of twice a day - so as to avoid electronic 'piles'. In some organisations, messages are automatically erased after a few hours if individuals have not checked them - the idea is to prompt people into a discipline, and it works! If you are away from your office, log in regularly.

- Avoid glare. Tilt the screen at an angle so that the bottom is lifted slightly towards you.

- Avoid working in the dark with only the screen as a source of light.

- If someone has sent you a document with a font size too small or difficult to read, change it.

- Rest your eyes by doing some exercises. Close your eyes for a full minute and imagine the colour black. Put the palm of your hands over your eyes to help see darkness. Or go to a window and stare at one point far in the distance for five seconds, and then without moving your head stare for five seconds at the nearest point to you. Repeat every 20 minutes or so.

- Schedule your day to take breaks at least every hour to relax the body. Do other tasks, for example make a telephone call or go to see somebody.

■ Sit on an adjustable chair that will support the small of your back.

Conversely, when you send a message electronically, think of the recipient. Here are a few tips to write better, electronically, and avoid being the generator of bumf.

## Twelve easy steps to writing an email

■ Agree with your team on a protocol to help individuals manage their messages. This might include what type of information will email be used for and a system for prioritising resulting actions.

■ Do you need to write this note? Would a phone call or a meeting be more efficient?

■ Keep your notes short. One screen length, if you can. Email memos are not designed to debate facts; they are designed to convey facts.

■ Simplify - keep the message simple and to the point. Do not use the traditional long heading used for written memos.

■ Consistency is essential in preparation and use of words.

■ Avoid repeating the sender's message back. If you reply to a message, it is a waste of the recipient's time to include the full original message followed by 'OK' at the top or bottom.

■ Pause before hitting the 'Reply All' button: you are wasting most of these people's time. One person's information is another person's bumf.

■ If you are writing a short message, capitals are the equivalent of shouting at someone.

■ Leave gaps between paragraphs.

■ Do not send your message to people who do not need it. The abuse of copying clutters other people's in-boxes with your bumf.

■ Do not dump your emails in large electronic filing cabinets - the retrieval will prove difficult

■ Apply the twice-a-year rule - tidy up your files twice a year, eliminating about 70%. Disk storage is expensive.

One of the benefits of email is its informality and speed. Over the years, a new short form of phrases have gained popular usage. Here are some:

| | |
|---|---|
| BCNU | Be seeing you |
| BTW | By the way |
| FWIW | For what it's worth |
| F2F | Face to face |
| FYI | For your information |
| IMHO | In my humble opinion |
| TTYL | Talk to you later |

But of course there is more to using technology than brushing up one's skills or technique. With the advance of communications via computer, the nature of one's work is radically changed. Two areas are affected: one is loss of individuality, the other is a reinforced centralisation.

This is why in Richard's case, he should organise a protocol to establish what has to be sent by email, who is to be copied, and re-instate other modes of communications. This would abolish unnecessary copying. And a colleague a few yards away would probably benefit from talking to Richard face to face rather than sending an email.

Also, filters exist. These electronic personal assistants are sophisticated enough to filter things out. Simply enter the keywords of the subjects you do not want to read about, and presto, the filter will not allow it to clutter your in-box. Richard would do well to ask his IT department to install such a system to avoid spam. There are several very reliable systems available that will, for a few pounds, install a spam killer, a personal security system, an anti-virus program and a firewall.

But not every example is a bad story, I have come across one large organisation which introduced its staff to the efficiency of IT skilfully. Here is the abridged story.

---

### *Bumf, Culture and Information Technology*

In the mid-1980s, a blue-chip multinational was about to move from scattered offices to a prestigious, centralised building. Part of the policy behind the move was to introduce information technology in each department. Until then, it had been a haphazard affair. Each employee was to have a PC and was meant to use it. Before the move, courses were organised to allow those who needed to catch up with typing skills, computer literacy and so on. A week after the move was completed, the Managing Director called in his most senior colleagues and demonstrated how to use the machine. He then exhorted his colleagues to pass the message on down the line. They did so. Within two months two thousand staff had abandoned the old way of doing things. All were using their newly installed technology.

For the visitor, this presented an extraordinary contrast. One arrived on a floor and the most striking feature was the silence. Office doors were open, hut no one seemed to talk. People were sitting at keyboards, peering at screens. Telephone usage was halved, meetings reduced in number: people used the electronic mail system. And yet, human contact had been preserved.

A large cafe area had been installed, complete with waitress service. Staff could sit down or, continental style, stand at the bar.

The noise in the bar was phenomenal. People were having face-to-face exchanges over a hot chocolate or an expresso. The office had become an efficient, silent working place. The paperless bumf happened in the cafe!

---

Over the years, the company has introduced protocols to avoid cluttering electronic 'wires' and taken some measures to remind people that the intranet and emails require as much discipline as the old-fashioned post. For example, incoming emails are erased if they are not read within a week. If people go on a business trip, or on holiday, they can request that the emails are saved. Filters are widely available to stamp out spam or to sort out incoming mail. People working in that organisation use all the facilities on offer as it does help them reduce bumf.

A report published in 2003 by Continental Research discloses that only 16 per cent of large businesses with a turnover of more than £5m have policies in place forbidding staff from using the Internet for personal reasons. Most companies are likely to have a policy in place on staff use of the Internet and generally request that personal Internet use should not interfere with work.

## Hands-on exercises

☞　If you have several piles of bumf, simplify them into two piles as described in this chapter. Discard the remainder now!

☞　Become more alert to the need to attend meetings. Could you drop out of a regular one while being informed of its outcome?

☞　Could you save time by delegating the attendance to some meetings? Consider junior people who need to be exposed to all kinds of situations.

☞　Reflect on the last meeting you chaired, how could you reduce its bumf?

*41*

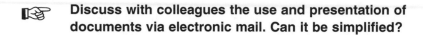

☞ **Discuss with colleagues the use and presentation of documents via electronic mail. Can it be simplified?**

☞ **Set up a protocol about your intranet.**

# 3

# Bin Your Bumf

UNSOLICITED MAIL FACTS

LIMIT YOUR INFORMATION COLLECTION

GUT MAGAZINES

HANDS-ON EXERCISES

## Unsolicited mail facts

You may not be surprised to learn that the average UK business person receives 14 items of direct mail each week. Of the 588 million items of business direct mail sent out by suppliers, about 2% generated business, but throwing away 61% of this vast amount consumed a significant amount of business time, especially as some of it was read before it was thrown away.

Be careful if you purchase goods by post. At the end of the order form you will see, in small print of course, a question asking you whether you permit the supplier to pass your name and address to other suppliers. If you do not, you need to tick the box. Nothing is easy! Similarly, the Electoral Register will ask you, from time to time, whether you authorise them to pass on your particulars to prospective suppliers. If you do not want to be inundated with unwanted bumf, fill the form.

*43*

# Limit your information collection

---

## *A Cautionary Tale*

During recessionary times The Sales Director of a company manufacturing concrete products for the construction industry had an idea. Why not enter another sector of the concrete product business, diversify, extend the product range into fancy garden paving, decorative tubs, concrete fencing and concrete garden furniture? The idea seemed great. A whole new market opened up in his mind.

The first morning back in the office he instructed some of his staff to find out all they could about concrete 'garden' products made for the retail market garden centres, builders and do-it-yourself merchants. What sort of products were already on sale? What prices, designs, type of sales inducements? Within a few days, diligent staff reappeared with an astonishingly large volume of brochures, pamphlets and price lists.

This rang an alarm hell in the Sales Director's head. He called the library enquiry desk of his trade association. Please could they let him have the trade breakdown figures for the 'domestic' or DIY sector of the concrete products business? A day or two later a few pages of information appeared on his desk. It showed that the market was saturated with manufacturers, with an enormous range of products and qualities. Competition was cut-throat in garden DIY products. And compared with the wholesale construction industry, the DIY industry was a pygmy. Obviously, it was not worth fighting for a segment of a small market, but far better to put renewed effort into their main market, and try to find some innovative new products or marketing or quality improvement methods there.

---

Collecting information without a clear objective works against more important information for which a clear requirement exists. All the information except the last two or three sheets collected by the Sales Director above was a waste of time. His first enquiry should have been to his trade association. The first question should have been 'What is the status of the garden products market?' before getting down to the nitty-gritty of what products there were and how much they cost. The anecdote describes an attitude of mind which believes that to take decisions, one needs to assemble as much information as possible. 'The more information one has to evaluate, the less one knows,' says Marshall McLuhan, a communication theorist. What is needed, in fact, is to gather only the relevant or necessary information. Here are four rules to avoid information overload:

■ Ask yourself what type of information you really need. Think in terms of purpose, not accumulation. Reading too much data can cloud a manager's judgement and slow down the decision-making process.

■ Be critical of raw statistics and measurements, like the typical 1.2 children per family in some countries, or the public opinion poll which indicates that 64.73% of people have a certain view, when only 1,000 people were questioned. Such accuracy may be useful for your purpose, but takes significant effort to produce. Inaccuracy may be more common: either the methods of measurement are wrong, or an error has occurred or a set of figures ignores something that has changed. For example, there was a time when people believed that all cholesterol was bad. But what is important about cholesterol is the proportion of HDL (high density lipoprotein, 'good' cholesterol) to LDL (low density lipoprotein, 'bad' cholesterol).

■ Network or discuss with people who have specialist knowledge. They have already collected the data and can give you meaningful information.

■ Keep a wide range of information sources open. If you ask yourself 'What will I do with the information?' you will find that you will make links between a variety of items that you learn and many of those items you already know. A wide range of information sources encourages you to think and mull ideas around; thinking makes you better informed.

# Gut magazines

Are you one of these people who uses commuting time to good effect by reading magazines and journals in the train or underground? Well done! But what about the time it takes you to find what you want among all those pages, and what about the weight of what you carry back and forth?

The proportion of advertising material to articles in magazines is surprising (see Figure 3.1). Some typical issues of magazines and journals contain the following amounts of advertising.

- A typical issue of *The Economist* - 42% of its pages
- *Chemistry in Britain* - 38% of its contents
- *The Director*, published by the Institute of Directors - 36%
- The Institute of Management journal *Management Today* - 42%

To reduce your article search time (and your luggage weight) tear the advertising bumf out of your magazines and keep the rest. But if you are interested in only one or two articles in the magazine after you have skimmed through the table of contents and flicked through the summary or first paragraph of all articles, tear those articles out of the magazine.

If you cannot tear up a magazine because it is a circulation copy or belongs to someone else, get someone to photocopy the articles you are interested in, and pass it on quickly to minimise the amount of bumf on your desk.

## Ratios in the average business magazine

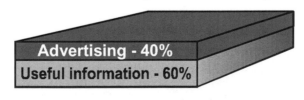

*Figure 3.1 - Advertising bumf in magazines*

## Hands-on exercises

☞ Can you delegate sifting through unsolicited mail to an assistant?

☞ Decide what you are at present interested in. Does it really require buying more books, or joining more clubs or institutes? Your bumf may be reduced by 70%.

☞ Use the services offered by the Royal Mail and the telephone companies to filter and stop unsolicited post or messages.

☞ Stop people in meetings who go into unnecessary detail or throw in figures that are not relevant to the subject under discussion.

☞ Practice gutting your own personal magazines.

# 4

# Beat Your Bumf Blockages

REDUCE PROCRASTINATION AND
INTERRUPTIONS

DEAL WITH OBSTINATE VISITORS

IMPROVE MEMORY AND RECALL

USE RECALL PATTERNS

HANDS-ON EXERCISES

## Case Study

Alison is an academic in a small language department in a London College. She tends to make lists of things to do. Today, she has minutes of meetings to read and correct, a paper from a colleague to comment on, several unpalatable decisions to take about a couple of students, a couple of phone calls to chase a grant application she made some time ago and, for her own research, there is a mounting pile of international papers gathered, but unread, over the last few weeks. But today is only Tuesday and she thinks 'I have the rest of the week to deal with them'. Wednesday goes by: Alison adds more to the list. Thursday arrives. Alison wants to begin the day tackling the first item on her list. But a voice in her head says, 'Are you sure you won't get interrupted? Shouldn't you chase up yesterday's unfinished business first? What about making the phone calls while you have the time? And check your

your email? Besides, you have all of tomorrow for these wretched minutes.' 'That's quite true,' thinks Barbara 'I'll do it then' 'But what about the students?' says another voice. 'Oh well,' she replies, 'they are not here right now, I'd better wait until I see them.'

In the meantime, two of her colleagues are infuriated by her habit of postponing decisions. They complain bitterly behind her back: 'She has all the information she needs. Now is the time to take a decision but, once more, she'll wait until tomorrow and then ask us to provide unnecessary work.'

On Friday morning, Alison has to deal with an unforeseen crisis. A colleague is off sick and she has to take his class and teach. It takes most of her time to prepare and deliver the lecture. By four o'clock, Alison is tired and cross with herself. 'I just have no self-discipline; it is a vicious circle. I'll have to look at these papers over the weekend. What a way to begin the weekend!'

Alison is a procrastinator, enduring life rather than enjoying it, caught in the spiral of never having enough time to do things, or having enough information to take decisions. She does not set a specific time to achieve tasks and excludes what she does not like from her schedule. Though it is difficult for someone like Alison to change her habits, there are many ways she can regain control of her life and strengthen defence against bumf.

# Reduce procrastination and interruptions

Slow readers like Alison and those faced with an unpleasant reading task tend to put off reading as much as they can, for as long as they can. If you belong to this group, you need to understand the reasons for your behaviour. It is because either:

- you perceive reading as an unpleasant, long, tiresome task, or
- the material is complex and overwhelming and you may not know how and where to start.

If the material is complex and overwhelming, it should help if you follow some of these rules.

☑ **Start now**. Remember the Chinese proverb: *'A 1,000 mile march starts with the first step'*. The 'now effect' reduces the gap between thought and action. Plunge right in; don't listen to inner voices that are tempting you away.

☑ Divide the material into **chunks**. Concentrated 20-minute bits throughout the morning are better than spending a whole morning on something that should have taken one hour.

☑ Give yourself **deadlines**. If you are researching for something, set a time to finish reading three of the papers, or chapters. If you receive reports, which day of the week will you circulate them, or send them to the central filing system? Enter your self-imposed deadlines in your diary or on your list of jobs for today, as you would with other appointments and engagements. Set definite starting and finishing times for particular reading tasks. Get a clock or timer and set it.

☑ **Involve** a colleague if possible. Say you are researching this or that, or that you need to make a decision on this or that report and you would like their opinion when you have read it. Set a time for your work together.

☑ **Congratulate** yourself as you are moving along. Consider what you have achieved and that it is not so complicated after all. (This is another reason why breaking the material into chunks is helpful.)

Preparation for serious reading means getting ready mentally. Beware of interruptions or, more insidiously, waiting or expecting to be distracted. Sometimes we create our own interruptions; often the greatest culprit is ourselves. Faced with an unpleasant task, how often have you given yourself the excuse of calling someone with no good reason, to deal with a low priority query, or just for a chat, and interrupting that person! Or have you ever been thinking 'there is no point in my starting this now, I am bound to be interrupted as soon as

I start', and sure enough, you are and you rejoice! Interruptions can be controlled. To reduce their negative effects, here are some guidelines. Don't be your own worst enemy: if you recognise yourself in the paragraph above, decide to do something about it.

☑ Tell others that you need to study a document and do not want to be disturbed.

☑ If you have an 'open door' policy, shut it when you need time to yourself. One to two hours per day is reasonable.

☑ Ask your secretary or a colleague to take phone calls and to discourage visitors for the time you need.

☑ Find a quiet place or office for, say, one hour, and do not tell anyone where you are.

☑ Come to the office early in the morning, before the phones start ringing or people are in, one day a week and get on with your reading. Alternatively, stay late one day a week. Early is best, because your mind and the day are fresh.

## Deal with obstinate visitors

If people ignore your message that you wish to be undisturbed, stand up when they approach your desk. Someone perceived to be on the move gives the message that he or she is in a hurry. Don't sit down. Ask how long their query will last. If more than five minutes, refuse to discuss it now. Say that your mind is on something else and that their problem requires your full attention. Make an appointment that is mutually convenient. Avoid eye contact from now on and firmly accompany the person out of the room.

# Improve memory and recall

Many people blame their memory. They say, 'I seem to remember trivia,' or 'Soon after a meeting, I can't remember what people have said.' And, 'I have to write everything down, otherwise, I do not take anything in,' and also, 'I go to a room and I have forgotten what I want there.' Such a waste of time, so much bumf written down and so much unnecessary effort dissipated in return for little reward. The final straw is the comment 'As I get older, my memory is getting worse.' Part of your defence to beat the bumf is to develop a better memory system.

*'If you want things to stay as they are, things will have to change,'* wrote Giuseppe di Lampedusa. Do you remember when he wrote? Here is a clue: it became a film in the 1970s with Burt Lancaster and Claudia Cardinale. No? Well, Guiseppe's name itself gives you something to work on - Italian isn't it? Or something close to it. Yes, that's it, you are getting close. Sicily, I hear? Spot on. Of course, you are right: 'The Leopard'. Well done. If you knew this, but it did not come back, what can you do? In my view, your best defence against bumf is to **maximise your memory**.

Imagine your memory as a filing cabinet with a couple of drawers containing the right amount of files, neatly ordered. Someone asks you a question: you open the appropriate drawer, pick up the correct file and provide the answer. Unfortunately people's memory is not always so carefully organised. Someone asks a question: you open a drawer at random and find nothing relevant there, or the file is missing and you have a blank - literally!

To explain and remedy the problem we need to examine memory a little.

### Memory consists of taking in information, storing it and retrieving it.

Memory is the ability to recreate what was. Psychologists further divide memory into working or short-term memory and long-term memory.

## How do we create what was?

Everything in memory begins with the senses. That is how we take in information. We see something, hear it, touch it, taste it or smell it. When we say we do not remember what was said at a meeting, it is probably because, at the time, our mind wandered off. We heard voices, but did not *actively listen* to what they said. Similarly, if you go to an exhibition and recall vividly a couple of paintings, it is because you paid active attention to them - unlike the other fifty or so which were seen, but not registered.

The senses play the initial part - interest and emotions secure your memory. This is crucial as we get older: we tend to be less interested in certain things, or to lack the enthusiasm or loathing towards them. This is detrimental to maintaining a healthy memory. I meet many people who say they cannot remember people's names. Questioned further, they admit in not being really interested in these people. First problem. Secondly, as they are not interested, they have no feeling towards the person they are meeting. As a result, they do not listen actively to the name when they first hear it. If the name is not taken in, the drawer and file are empty. Do not waste your time looking for it! So, to remedy this, brush up on your senses and get interested.

## Brushing up your senses

The single biggest reason people do not remember is that they do not pay attention. Can you recall the taste of your coffee today? What a friend wore yesterday? What your partner's shoes look like now? If your senses are not alert, they do not register relevant information. So, first, be alert, engaging all your senses. Simultaneously, create a mental snapshot of what you are taking in. These conscious actions will trigger an active selection and mental process towards what you want to remember. Incidentally this is what working - or short-term - memory is about - being actively engaged with what you want to remember. Here, I highly recommend Dr Gary Small's (13) book to set you on a complete programme to improve your memory.

## Getting interested

First you make sure that the information goes in, otherwise it certainly will not be retrieved! Do you frequently suffer from total memory loss after, say, one hour of learning something? This is probably a remnant of the school system which emphasised cramming information to pass exams at the expense of raising an interest in the subject. Before you take in information and, therefore, remember it, there must be interest. You need to stimulate your curiosity. Try to attune past experience to the new knowledge in front of you.

Some people confuse interest and obligations. Think of the things you do not remember - are they a cause of anxiety? Why do you want to remember them? Is it because you feel guilty about not knowing them, or you think someone of your status should know about such things?

Getting interested in something becomes easier as one gets older. Why? Because:

- unlike the novice or the young person, you have accumulated a bank of knowledge on which you can build; you are not starting from scratch with few landmarks to guide your new knowledge.
- you are clearer about what is important to you and what is not; choices and selectivity are easier
- you are no longer on trial or have to pass exams; you can afford to say 1 do not know' about something.

## Short-term memory

Short-term memory is easily overloaded. For example, if you are listening to a speech or watching a movie and someone asked you to repeat word for word what you had heard in the last two minutes, you would probably find the task difficult: you were not paying attention to all the details. However, if the person were to ask you what the speech or movie was about, you would probably be able to reply quite easily. Paying attention to what you are doing is what short-term memory is about. As such, it has its limitations. George A Miller was the first psychologist to report that the mind can handle 'seven plus-or-minus two' concepts, letters, digits as in telephone numbers, postal codes, anagrams, ideas central to a book, and so on, without extra help like notes.

Short-term memory can be made more efficient if we reorganise or chunk the material. For example, if you are trying to memorise the contents of a manual, it will be easier and more productive if you memorise the titles or main ideas of chapters, say eight of them, rather than the first eight lines of important text in the manual.

Now fill each chunk with meaning. Meaning, as we discussed in Chapter I, goes far beyond the visual recognition of words. *Meaningful material* relates to your past knowledge and experience, and expectations of what you want to extract. This is what experts call **encoding**. For example, can you name the Great Lakes of North America in 30 seconds? The answer (at the foot of page - but don't cheat!) shows how useful encoding is.

## Long-term memory

Most people blame their long-term memory - recall is not as speedy as they would like, or as accurate, or it is simply not there. To correct this, after the information is encoded properly, we need to consolidate this information. This can take the form of repetition, rehearsal or thinking about the new information. For example, you are at a meeting and you are alert - try encoding by taking a mental snapshot of what people are saying. What is needed now is consolidation. As you walk back to your office, retrace how you felt when people said certain things. By the time you reach your desk, your brain will be ready to organise this information. The information will find its way into the right file in your brain.

Long-term memory is an organised, structured databank of knowledge, like the filing cabinet described earlier. It is organisation

The Great Lakes - remember HOMES - Huron, Ontario, Michigan, Erie, Superior that makes retrieval and recall possible. There are many techniques available to help organise information, from using a diary to mastering **mnemonics** (an aid to memory).They are all based on the following principle. We link the unknown (the new information we are learning and trying to remember) to the known (what we have accumulated over the years). In mnemonics, the link is done by making an unusual mental image. The illustration show you how this works.

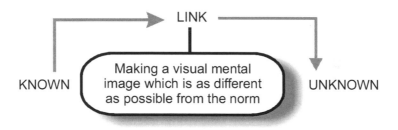

*Figure 4.1 - The principle behind mnemonics*

## Mnemonics

Mnemonics work on the principle shown in figure 4.1. To show how the principle works, take for example, the need to recall the ten sections of a report you have to present. Start by thinking, for example, about your house or flat (the known). The purpose at the moment is to find ten different locations which are, to you, in a logical sequence. You may start with your front door. Mentally, re-acquaint yourself with it (take information in). Does it need repairing? Is the surface rough or smooth? Do you like it? Move to the second location, say, the hall. Mentally re-acquaint yourself with it. If you switch the light on, is it bright or dull? Is the effect of the decoration pleasing? Warm? Is there an object there you particularly like? Now move to the third location, which to you is a logical sequence. Examine the room or place again, as before. Take your time.

Now, let's work out how to memorise the contents of the report with its ten sections - say, Recession, Recovery, Interest rates, Unemployment, etc. Can you make a simple mental picture that represents each one? Recession could be an empty factory, while Recovery is a full order book. Now, all you need to do is to link the **unknown** (the ten sections of the report) to the **known** (your house). The first section is Recession represented by an empty factory. Can you see your front door opening onto an empty factory? Now the second section, Recovery, represented by a full order book. Can you see in your hall, instead of a rug or a piece of furniture, a huge order book which people sign as they come in? And so on until you have linked the ten sections of the report to things you know well, in a specific order.

This memory aid technique has been in use since ancient Greek orators used it to memorise their speeches.

---

### *One way to describe recall*

Douglas Hofstadter, in his brilliant hook *Metamagical Themas: Questing for the Essence of Mind and Pattern* (2), reminds us of the mathematician Stan Ulam's theory about retrieval. When Ulam was searching for a piece of information that eluded him, he sent 'ten sniffing dogs' after it. The metaphor was to release the dogs in his brain and let them go sniffing in parallel. While some would go into the wrong alleyways, another would bring back the desired piece. Now, have you not. on occasions, read something which you are trying to recall? And you say, hold on, it was last week, no - last month - that's right - I was on the train to Birmingham. Oh, I know, it was in that magazine about ... The dogs are searching and when they are on the wrong path you send them back. It is interesting that we just need a small cue to retrieve the entire material. A whiff will do!

---

Psychologists have long known that retention of knowledge decreases with time, particularly if the knowledge is not revised or used. The graph in Figure 4.2 illustrates how retention and recall ability decays. However, given the correct stimulus, we can remember everything.

This shows that we retain perfectly what we do every day; the problem starts when we try to retrieve or recall this information.

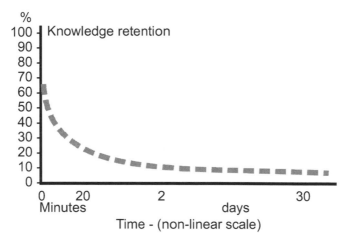

*Figure 4.2 - How retention and recall ability decays*

Why do we forget? 'The easiest answer is, we don't,' writes Professor JZ Young (12). We have many subconscious memories. The problem lies in the fact that we have not yet mastered a system for retrieving them.

## Use recall patterns

If a meeting is complex, or you need to make a presentation and find that copious notes are unnecessary bumf that distract you, consider the use of Recall Patterns. Tony Buzan, (14) calls them Mind Maps®. The principles are simple:

- Write the main idea or subject in the centre of the page.
- Add associated ideas branching from the centre.
- Use keywords which summarise a train of thought.
- Write in capitals rather than in script, to aid legibility.

*59*

- Try to use a colour coding of related ideas, perhaps one colour per branch.

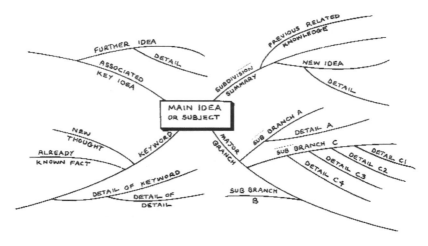

*Figure 4.3 - The basic Mind Map®*

The advantage of recall patterns over linear notes is that you organise the notes yourself and do not have to follow the author's plan. Thus it allows you to hook new pieces of information to old immediately, and enables you to tailor the information to the emphasis that you - rather than the author of the book - require.

You can buy a software package, 'The Mind Manager' published by Mindjet, to write a mind map electronically.

## Hands-on exercises

### Procrastination

 Reflect on the types of task you put off. Are they small tasks like filing? Or large like taking an important decision? What excuse do you use? How can you avoid the excuse?

## Interruptions

 Start a task: jot down how long it was before you were interrupted. Reflect how you could have avoided the interruption.

## Memory

 Increase your interest by doing the following exercise. Look at a cup. Don't just say - 'Okay, it's just a cup - an ordinary cup.' Rediscover the cup for the next two minutes:

- If you hold it in your hand is it hot, cold, pleasing, rough, smooth?
- Is it greyish, yellowish . . .?
- Does it have a rim at the bottom?
- Is it marked, chipped or crazed?
- Can you put one or two fingers through the handle?

One hour later, without looking at the cup, recall all the features of the cup. Repeat the exercise the next day with a pen, a shoe and so on. Then a conversation you heard, a film you saw ...

 Make a recall Pattern of the News you watch on Television, as you hear them. Look at them the next day. Do they still make sense? Do they trigger more memories in your mind?

 If you are seriously interested in improving your memory, take a look at *'Improving Your Memory for Dummies'* (21)

# Part 2

## Offence against Bumf

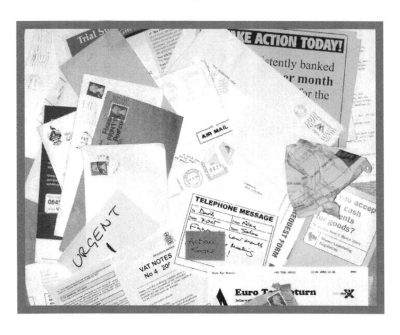

# 5

# Beat the Bumf

---

**THE NATURE OF BUMF PROBLEMS**

**WHAT TYPES OF INFORMATION SHOULD AN ORGANISATION DISSEMINATE?**

**HANDS-ON EXERCISES**

---

## The nature of bumf problems

The use of information technology - or the smart machine as some call it - is accelerating. But how instructive is the information or bumf you receive? Beware of dealing only with paper-driven information. Pay specific attention to computer technology-driven information. Computerised information, computer-controlled production and computer-controlled stock-taking systems are here to stay. The emergence of information technology has reduced dramatically the cost of assembling, reproducing and disseminating information.

Consequently, information has proliferated in many different formats such as magazines and periodicals, subscriber services, direct marketing, and cable and radio telecommunications facilities. You find you are on the mailing lists of organisations you never knew existed, bombarded with all sorts of offers, facts and data from all parts of the world. In your work, you receive piles of information, much of which is of little or no use to you. Are you receiving information or bumf?

Take your first offensive against bumf. Use a 'Bumf Log' as shown in Table 5.1 to identify and eliminate unwanted material, and fill it in as illustrated. This will help you determine where your bumf problems lie. When you have given the Bumf Log some time and thought, you will be well on the way to analysing the problem and have some ideas on how and where it should be tackled.

First, from where do you receive information? Consider all types of paperwork, electronic and other information (and misinformation) that reaches your desk. We'll call all these information sources the **bumf**.

Second, with what **frequency** are you subjected to a particular type of bumf:- several times per day or only once a year?

Third, what is your **need** for that bumf? How important is it to you? For example, you may be interested in only 10% of the contents of a particular computer database manual but that 10% is crucial for your job performance. So we have to weight the quantity estimate by describing the degree of importance of the information contained in the bumf source. So next to 'Need' we have **quantity**, which denotes what proportion of a particular document is of use to you.

Next, we have to consider the **purpose** for which you require the information. What arguments, ideas or actions will this reading prompt? Once absorbed, what will you do with this information? Will you mull it around in your head, prepare a presentation, incorporate it in a report, or give instructions?

And last, what **time** was **spent** working on each information source? How long did it take to dig out what you wanted from all the other irrelevant information?

Having looked at the Bumf Log example in Figure 5.1 (many of which items might well apply to you), now complete your particular requirements on Table 5.2.

*Figure 5.1 - The Bumf Log - opposite*

*Figure 5.2 - The Bumf Log - blank for completion - page 68*

| BUMF | FREQUENCY | NEED | QUANTITY | PURPOSE | TIME |
|---|---|---|---|---|---|
| Manuals | Annually | Crucial | 10% | To operate PC | 10 hrs/yr |
| Reports - internal/external | Quarterly | Very important | 75% | Explore alternatives | 6 hrs/wk |
| Memos | Weekly | Important | 50% | Receive instructions | 2 hrs/wk |
| Letters/ post | 6 per day | Sometimes | 25% | Take action | 10 hrs/wk |
| Meetings | Bi-weekly | Important | 100% | Take action | 6 hrs/wk |
| Minutes of meetings | Bi-weekly | Crucial | 25% | Coordinate action | 2 hrs/wk |
| Conference papers | Bi-annually | Sometimes | 50% | Keep up-to-date | 20 hrs/wk |
| Email | Daily | Crucial | 75% | Keep up-to-date | 5 hrs/wk |
| Books | 6 per year | Sometimes | 50% | Learn | 20 hrs/yr |
| Profesional magazines | Monthly | Sometimes | 40% | Keep up-to-date | 2 hrs/wk |
| Journals | Bi-monthly | Sometimes | 10% | Keep up-to-date | 2 hrs/wk |
| New spapers | Daily | Low | 25% | Keep up-to-date | 2 hrs/wk |
| Computer printouts | Daily | Important | 1% | Disseminate info | 1 hr/wk |
|  |  |  |  |  |  |
|  |  |  |  |  |  |
|  |  |  |  |  |  |
|  |  |  |  |  |  |

| BUMF | FREQUENCY | NEED | QUANTITY | PURPOSE | TIME |
|------|-----------|------|----------|---------|------|
|      |           |      |          |         |      |
|      |           |      |          |         |      |
|      |           |      |          |         |      |
|      |           |      |          |         |      |
|      |           |      |          |         |      |
|      |           |      |          |         |      |
|      |           |      |          |         |      |
|      |           |      |          |         |      |
|      |           |      |          |         |      |
|      |           |      |          |         |      |
|      |           |      |          |         |      |
|      |           |      |          |         |      |
|      |           |      |          |         |      |
|      |           |      |          |         |      |
|      |           |      |          |         |      |

From your consideration of various types of bumf and their relative importance for you on the Bumf Log (Table 5.2), you should now have a good idea of which documents you should read carefully, look through quickly, or which you can ignore. Be assertive and bin  unimportant documents or delete irrelevant emails or computer screen displays.

Do you see a bumf pattern emerging from Table 5.2, your own Bumf Log? If so, consult the list of bumf problems contained in the Introduction to this book. There you will find references to the answers.

Review this list in, say, six months' time, to check how much you have improved your ability to deal with bumf.

## What types of information should an organisation disseminate?

As an information giver, how often do we think about what the reader will do with the information or data we are disseminating?

---

### *Technical Bumf Case Study*

In the 1970s, computer manuals were written by boffins for boffins. They were so user-unfriendly (xenophobic) that they strengthened many people's fears about technology. Manuals are very different today. Their writers have learned the hard way that readers need to find information easily and that it must be meaningful. This means that they help readers to bridge the gap between new data and previous knowledge, to feel encouraged and not overwhelmed, to find what they need quickly and not feel guilty about what they leave out. Here is an example of an improved manual:

*'You should begin by reading Chapter I and trying some small exercises of your own. Go through Chapter 2 quickly, concentrating on the summaries and tables; don't get bogged down in details. Then read as far into each chapter as your interest takes you. The chapters are nearly independent of each other, so the order doesn't matter much.'* (16).

---

Similarly with meetings, do you complain that you are wasting time because meetings are proliferating, the topics overlap, the chairperson or participants digress too frequently or the meeting goes on for too long?

What has happened with meetings and paper may happen on-line, with electronically controlled information. Most businesses now use computers and related work-stations. As data collection, retrieval and dissemination are made easier through information technology, managers must restrain their appetite for more information, or work will soon drown in an excess of information.

But when you receive the 'correct' type of information, your work performance can be revolutionised. Professor Zuboff, writing in *The Age of the Smart Machine* (5), argues that some organisations may use information technology not only to 'automate' but also to 'informate' workers. She means empower workers with knowledge. As one worker she interviewed put it: 'If I can control my own access to data, I can control my own learning.' (p 237). This means improved performance for the benefit of the organisation. Viewed this way, information becomes accessible to all and enables all personnel to learn and gain insight.

Some organisations are transforming organisational life through initiatives like empowerment. They are pushing responsibility and information down to all levels in the organisation and making people responsible for their own work performance, career and personal growth. When people accept responsibility for their own access to and control of information, and share information wisely, they cut out the bumf.

A manager within an organisation must review the frequency, necessity and quantity of information that his or her team receives.

- Simplify and limit the information you generate and disseminate.
- Avoid any information that does not show a clear purpose.
- Scrutinise the need for formal meetings.
- Train people to run meetings efficiently.
- And remember, when was the last time you solved a problem by throwing data and statistics at it?

But it is a fine line between transmitting too much information and too little, as the following story illustrates.

J. Edgar Hoover, well known for the autocratic manner with which he ran the FBI in 1930s and 1940s, was a master of handling information. He insisted that all memos for his attention should summarise the message on one (and only one) A4 size sheet, with wide borders left around the edges of the paper for his comments and instructions. He received one such memo, concerning spies, but the borders were a little narrow. Amongst his comments he included 'Watch the borders', meaning make sure the margins on the memo were kept wide. Immediately the telegraph wires were humming all over the United States. 'Watch the borders' went out the urgent instruction to all frontiers, ports and airports from his well- trained staff.

---

### Retail Industry Case Study

Consider a large food retailer which sends daily, to each store manager, information covering about 100 A4 sheets. The information includes:
   o product lines discontinued and newly introduced
   o errors on earlier information lists and on product labelling
   o future special promotions and offers
   o supply forecasts
   o ordering advice
   o health and safety notices and reminders
   o limited availability of some products.

Store managers have many responsibilities involved with the smooth running of the store, which they enjoy. This does not leave much time free for reading piles of bumf, which they do not enjoy.
   If you were the director of information (information giver) what would you do to lighten the load on the store managers? To answer this question you need to put yourself into the position of a store manager (information receiver). You could:

---

- colour code the information pages, so that pages concerning groceries may be handed directly to the groceries manager, health and safety to the H & S manager, and so on
- prioritise information into immediate action items, and short and long-term future action information
- use a consistent set of icons on the information sheets to categorise items concerning, for instance, customers, errors, wrappings, internal communications, staff, reports, etc.
- divide the A4 sheets into columns to ease reading, as a newspaper is laid out
- check who really needs the information (i.e. prune standard distribution lists whenever possible) and who is the real recipient of the information. For instance, if it is a notice for the customer, send a notice already made out. Don't tell the store manager so that he has to have the notice made up.

## Hands-on exercises

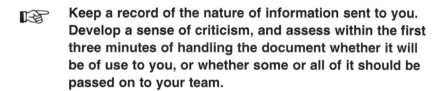 Keep a record of the nature of information sent to you. Develop a sense of criticism, and assess within the first three minutes of handling the document whether it will be of use to you, or whether some or all of it should be passed on to your team.

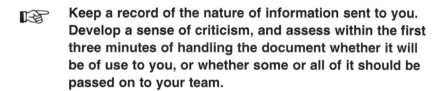 Before you send information to colleagues, ask yourself: Why? How much will they need?

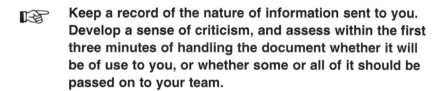 Discuss with colleagues or subordinates the value of some meetings.

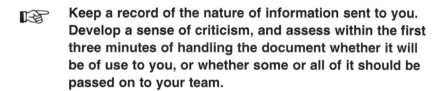 As a manager, ask colleagues if or how information received has prompted some to make better or faster decisions. If not, why not?

**As a receiver of information, discuss with the sender how bumf (irrelevant information) could be stripped away from the information you really need to receive.**

# 6

# Improve Your Reading

---

**GET RID OF MYTHS ABOUT READING**

**ESTIMATE YOUR READING SPEED**

**CHECK YOUR COMPREHENSION AND READING HABITS**

**IMPROVE YOUR CONCENTRATION**

**REDUCE THE EFFECTS OF DYSLEXIA**

**HANDS-ON EXERCISES**

---

This chapter is concerned with anything that stops you getting to the information that you really need. Part of the Offensive against bumf is to acknowledge your attitude towards reading, in particular when you confront uninviting documents.

## Get rid of myths about reading

There are many myths surrounding the reading process.

### Myth - reading for pleasure and work has to be slow

There is no evidence to support this view at all. Slow readers, in fact, find pleasure-reading too time-consuming to be enjoyable. This, of course, makes such readers reluctant even to start. Slow reading discourages the reader because there are so few early rewards. Slow readers get a fragmented comprehension. They miss the overall driving idea and meaning of the material, in the same way that a copy-typist who necessarily reads every word may not take in what she types. Her mind wanders off because reading is at the pace of typing - slow and dull. Slow readers tend to have poor concentration, as their minds wander off. This is because their brains are not fully engaged, get bored, and start drifting into competing thoughts.

## Myth - when you fail to comprehend or lose concentration, immediately re-read

This is one of the most common faults of poor readers - going back to check what you have just read, to try to gain understanding. It is very inefficient. It slows you down. It allows your mind to wander off. It sidetracks you from anticipating what is coming. It distracts you from thinking actively.

A simple technique for increasing comprehension and concentration is to maintain a dialogue with the author. Ask questions: why did he say that? Is it different from what he said before? Anticipate what the author will say in the next section of the document.

## Myth - reading is boring

This myth is popular with those who believe in myths 1 and 2. Reading is fun and rewarding if you are motivated, follow a rhythm and actively seek information. Reading fast, understanding it and retaining what is read are even more exciting.

## Myth - scanning can't be reading

Scanning is reading. It is the technique to apply when you are looking for something specific and you want to gain an overview of a whole document. Scanning is taking mental note of the presentation of material, picking up what stands out and reading headings and keywords. It is a vital part of efficient reading, sometimes used by itself, but more often in conjunction with other steps (see Chapters 7 and 8).

## Myth - you need long periods of time

You don't. If you know how to skim, you can pick up ideas from any document, effectively, in five minutes. But efficient and rapid reading requires concentration. You need to concentrate as soon as you decide to read. When you know what your objectives are, reading can be done in five or fifteen minute slots. Long periods spent reading do not necessarily mean efficient reading.

## Myth - technical documents can't be read rapidly

Such documents lend themselves very well to rapid reading. In most cases, they give background information which the reader may not need, at least to begin with. Efficient reading is a series of steps. The key step, in the case of technical reports, is to decide beforehand what you are seeking. Then scan the material, slowing down when you locate important passages. Of course, there will be more solid material in such documents than in a novel. To master the skill of efficient reading is to master flexibility - that is, use different speeds for different materials.

## Myth - when you read you need to remember everything

Put your efforts into making sense of the material. Over-anxiety about trying to remember it may damage your comprehension. Comprehension will take care of the need to memorise it. This myth is a symptom of insecurity. You know it is an impossible task, so you hide behind it. It allows you to say, 'I told you it was impossible. I can't do it.' You need to set achievable targets. Assess your familiarity with the subject and define your goals for this reading.

## Myth - you need to be an expert at everything

In a society that promotes education and bombards us with knowledge - be it legal, medical, political, or technical - we are afraid of appearing stupid. We pretend we know things we know little about and feel guilty if an area of ignorance is uncovered. Why? Resolve today to be selective. Remove the guilt. Remember that it is more important to know where to find information than to know everything.

# Estimate your reading speed

How do you read? Let's find out. The passage which follows will assess the speed at which you read, the extent of your comprehension, and the habits that you have. For this exercise to be of full value, please follow the instructions:

- Have ready a stopwatch or a watch with a second hand.
- Choose a comfortable place to read where you will not be interrupted.
- Try to read as you would normally - don't speed up or slow down because it is an exercise.
- Have a notebook by your side.
- Note the time when you start and when you finish reading the passage.
- Read the passage once only, from 'Quote' to 'Unquote'.

## *Quote ...*

As brisk as bees, if not altogether as light as fairies, did the four Pickwickians assemble on the morning of the twenty-second day of December, in the year of grace in which these, their faithfully-recorded adventures, were undertaken and accomplished. Christmas was close at hand, in all his bluff and hearty honesty; it was the season of hospitality, merriment and open-heartedness; the old year was preparing, like an ancient philosopher, to call his friends around him, and amidst the sound of feasting and revelry to pass gently and calmly away. Gay and merry was the time, and gay and merry were at least four of the numerous hearts that were gladdened by its coming.

And numerous indeed are the hearts to which Christmas brings a brief season of happiness and enjoyment. How many families, whose members have been dispersed and scattered far and wide, in the restless struggles of life, are then reunited, and meet once again in the happy state of companionship and mutual good-will, which is a source of such pure and unalloyed delight, and one so incompatible with the cares and sorrows of the world, that the religious belief of the most civilised nations, and the rude traditions of the roughest savages, alike number it among the first joys of a future condition of existence provided for the blest and happy! How many old recollections, and how many dormant sympathies, does Christmas time awaken!

We write these words now, many miles distant from the spot at which, year after year, we met on that day, a merry and joyous circle. Many of the hearts that throbbed so gaily then, have ceased to beat; many of the looks that shone so brightly then, have ceased to glow; the hands we grasped, have grown cold; the eyes we sought, have hid their lustre in the grave; and yet the old house, the room, the merry voices and smiling faces, the jest, the laugh, the most minute and trivial circumstances connected with those happy meetings, crowd upon our mind at each recurrence of the season, as if the last assemblage had been but yesterday! Happy, happy Christmas, that can win us back to the delusions of our childish days; that can recall to the old man the pleasures of his youth; that can transport the sailor and the traveller, thousands of miles away, back to his own fire-side and his quiet home!

But we are so taken up and occupied with the good qualities of this saint Christmas, that we are keeping Mr. Pickwick and his friends waiting in the cold on the outside of the Muggleton coach, which they have just attained, well wrapped up in great-coats, shawls and comforters. The portmanteaus and carpet-bags have been stowed away, and Mr. Weller and the guard are endeavouring to insinuate into the fore-boot a huge cod-flsh several sizes too large for it - which is snugly packed up, in a long brown basket, with a layer of straw over the top, and which has been left to the last, in order that he may repose in safety on the half-dozen barrels of real native oysters, all the property of Mr. Pickwick which have been arranged in regular order at the bottom of the receptacle. The interest displayed in Mr. Pickwick's countenance is most intense, as Mr. Weller and the guard try to squeeze the cod-fish into the boot, first head-first, and then tail-first, and then top upward, and then sideways, and then long-ways, all of which artifices the implacable cod-fish sturdily resists, until the guard accidentally hits him in the very middle of the basket, whereupon he suddenly disappears into the boot, and with him, the head and shoulders of the guard himself, who, not calculating upon so sudden a cessation of the passive resistance of the cod-fish, experiences a very unexpected shock, to the unsmotherable delight of all the porters and bystanders. Upon this, Mr. Pickwick smiles with great good-humour, and drawing a shilling from his waistcoat pocket, begs the guard, as he picks himself out of the boot, to drink his health in a glass of hot brandy and water: at which the guard smiles too, and Messrs. Snodgrass, Winkle, and Tupman, all smile in company. The guard and Mr. Weller disappear for five minutes: most probably to get the brandy and hot water, for they smell very strongly of it when they return, the coachman mounts the box, Mr. Weller jumps up behind. The Pickwickians pull their coats round their legs and their shawls over their noses, the helpers pull the horse-cloths off, the coachman shouts out a cheery 'All right,' and away they go.

They have rumbled through the streets, and jolted over the stones, and at length reach the wide and open country. The wheels skim over the hard and frosty ground: and the horses, bursting into a canter at a smart crack of the whip, step along the road as if the load behind them: coach, passengers, cod-fish, oyster barrels, and all: were but a feather at their heels. They have descended a gentle slope, and enter upon a level, as compact and dry as a solid block of marble, two miles long. Another crack of the whip, and on they speed, at a smart gallop: the horses tossing their heads and rattling the harness, as if in exhilaration at the rapidity of the motion: while the coachman, holding the whip and reins in one hand, takes off his hat with the other, and resting it on his knees, pulls out his handkerchief, and wipes his forehead: partly because he has a habit of doing it, and partly because it's as well to show the passengers how cool he is, and what an easy thing it is to drive four-in-hand, when you have had as much practice as he has. Having done this very leisurely (otherwise the effect would be materially impaired), he replaces the handkerchief, pulls on his hat, adjusts his gloves, squares his elbows, cracks his whip again, and on they speed, more merrily than before.

*... Unquote*

This extract is taken from *The Pickwick Papers* by Charles Dickens, Chapter XXVIII, A Good Humoured Christmas. There are 1,044 words in the passage.

Now let us consider how to calculate your reading speed. This is the formula to apply for this quotation passage.

### Speed = (Number of words in passage)/(minutes)

Say you took 4 minutes and 5 seconds to read this passage:

### 4 min 5 sec = (4+ 5/60) = 4.083 minutes

### Your reading speed = 1044/4.083 = 256 words per minute.

Or we can apply a general formula as another way to assess your reading speed. This approach is used when you read material that you have chosen, and you control the test reading time you wish to devote to it. You work out the average number of words per page from some sample pages where you have checked the typical number of lines per page and number of words per line.

### Speed or words per minute = (words per line) x (lines per page) x (pages read)/(time)

or

### Speed or words per minute = (words per page) x (pages read)/(time)

If you use this formula, you should select a reading time in advance and stop when it has elapsed. Choose 1, 2, 5 or 10 minutes for your test read. Use an alarm clock or kitchen timer to tell you when the set number of minutes has elapsed. If you stop reading three-quarters of the way down the page credit yourself with three-quarters of a page read. If your passage has a lot of short lines, use your judgement to make up full lines, and estimate the fraction of a page that it fills.

# Check your comprehension and reading habits

You are the best person to assess your reading comprehension. The questions to ask yourself about the passage you have just read (Dickens, *The Pickwick Papers*) to check your comprehension are:

**?** Have I got the general idea of what this passage was about?
**?** Is it sufficient for my present purpose?
**?** Am I missing some of the details? If so, does it matter?
**?** Do I understand enough of what I have read, so far, to continue?

For more mentally demanding 'reads' you may want to check some of the factors and techniques involved in improving comprehension by referring to the section on Reading and Understanding in Chapter 1.

In the passage from *The Pickwick Papers* that you read, did you notice any of the following habits:

| | | | |
|---|---|---|---|
| **?** | Hear the words in your head as you read (subvocalise)? | yes | no |
| **?** | Read one word at a time? | yes | no |
| **?** | Go back and re-read because you lost the meaning? | yes | no |
| **?** | Have problems remembering what it was about? | yes | no |
| **?** | Experience difficulty in maintaining your focus on the page? | yes | no |
| **?** | Find that your concentration wandered off? | yes | no |

If you have more than one bad habit - the number of 'yeses' in the list above - list them in order of their severity for you and go to the chapters in this book that deal specifically with them. Read only those sections that you do need to make you a rapid reader. Practice skimming now.

### Do you hear the words in your head?

Subvocalisation is hearing the words in your head, or saying the words to yourself as you read them. All readers do this to some degree. For example, if you are not a trained lawyer and need to read a contract, you will probably read it slowly, word for word. You are unfamiliar with the terminology and your eyes will take longer to recognise the words while your brain will be slower at decoding their meaning. You may even read some words or groups of words aloud. This is the extreme case of subvocalisation. If it is occasional and necessary for your understanding, do not worry about it. If, however, you subvocalise frequently, with familiar material, you have developed a bad habit and need to understand why.

When you learned to read, you said each word aloud to reinforce the relationship this particular order of letters conveyed as that particular word. Later, as you gained speed, reading aloud was discouraged. But some readers never lose this checking mechanism. They were not taught to modify their reading habits. They, particularly, were not taught to read words in a group, rather than singly. A fluent reader does not need to hear the words to understand the meaning of what he or she reads.

Another aspect of subvocalisation may be linked to how much you read and, consequently, the vocabulary you can recognise easily. If you do not read much, your reading vocabulary - that is pattern recognition - remains at a child's level. Read more, your vocabulary expands and the pattern recognition of these words becomes easier. *The Times* on March 22, 2002, reported a survey about the number of words used by famous authors. Shakespeare figures, of course, but also do Charles Dickens and Jane Austen. Amongst several others, Jane Austen used the least number of words in her novels; - about 7,000, while, perhaps surprisingly, Colin Dexter - of Inspector Morse fame - used just under 10,000. The more you read, the more varied the sources, the greater the ease of pattern recognition. (This is explained in the next chapter.)Consequently, your subvocalisation decreases.

Reducing subvocalisation is easy, but requires application. If, for example, in the speed exercise you achieved a speed of 200 words per minute and you want to double it, you have to drop some subvocalisation. You simply must force yourself to read faster. Then you won't have time to 'hear' the words. At first, you may feel a little disorientated. You will feel that you do not understand what you are

*83*

reading. But persevere and trust yourself!

As you gain speed, you will find that you are converting the sounds into pictures - as images. We have the ability to visualise. When reading and visualisation are combined, your speed and your comprehension are high.

---

### *Examples of subvocalisation*

If you read in a foreign language, subvocalisation tends to occur more frequently than in your mother tongue. This is because at a young age you did not learn to read these sets of letters side by side. Consequently it takes longer for the brain to decode such letters and the words. For example, in 'les cheveux de cet enfant', 'les liens de parente', 'votre lieu d'habitation', the letters 'eux' 'ien' and 'ieu', frequent in French, are rarely positioned side by side in English.

Similarly, if you embark on new studies or radically change jobs, you may be unsettled by new phraseology and terms. Subvocalisation may momentarily help you understand what you read.

In both cases - foreign language and a new vocabulary for you - decide first to familiarise yourself with as many new words as you can so as to lose their 'surprising' effect. When you think you have done so, force yourself to read faster and transform the words into images.

---

To practise visualisation, start with simple words. When you see the word 'house', picture in your mind a house. As you get better at visualisation, words describing abstracts will literally become shapes, colours or pictures in the same way as concrete words. For example, can you form a simple picture for partnership? How about two rings interlocked, or an elderly married couple? What about socialism? Perhaps a tall figure handing something to a smaller figure. Capitalism? Uncle Sam with bulging pockets! Visualisation is strongly linked to memory. We memorise events, ideas, concept better if we can see them in our minds. For more on memory, see Chapter 4.

# Improve your concentration

---

### *Case Study*

David is an ambitious, energetic engineer. He likes to be 'where the action is'. He enjoys meetings, he is quick at making decisions, he is supportive of his colleagues. But he has to read reports from Head Office. He tends to put reading off, but today, he has decided he cannot put this one off any longer. David picks up the report. After a casual glance through it, he searches in his file for some background information which he reads. He gets up, goes to the window and comes back to his desk to make a phone call.

He now starts on the report, but it is heavy going. He thinks how dull and poorly presented this information is and he misses important points. David looks at his watch and gets flustered because time is passing. He re-reads the last page that he read and continues.

After twenty minutes or so, David stops reading because he has reached a particularly boring passage. He looks at his emails and quickly responds. He closes the report and decides to go back to it after lunch. After lunch, David flicks through the report again and thinks: pity that it has not changed in the meantime! How could David break this self-defeating cycle?

---

If you reach the bottom of a page and do not remember what you have read, your concentration is poor. You have allowed your mind to wander off; you have given in to distractions. External distractions can be greatly reduced if you minimise disruptions as suggested earlier. Internal distractions depend largely on your previous experience of reading similar documents, your general level of knowledge about the subject you are tackling and the nature of the material. People who tend to re-read paragraphs or pages because of poor concentration take the lazy way out. They are not consciously thinking about reading the first time round. To break this cycle you can do several things.

- Refuse to re-read or regress as it is properly called.
- Read critically, with a purpose in mind. This is developed in Chapter 8, under Set Objectives.
- Use your power of anticipation. Try to anticipate the material you have yet to read. Try to foresee where the writer is taking you, how the report is progressing.
- Get involved. Don't read passively; have a dialogue with the writer, agree or disagree openly as you read.
- Don't fight your short concentration span: work with it. Every fifteen minutes, take small breaks. As you come back to the material, recall what you have read so far. Make some notes from memory.

Physical factors like the environment also affect concentration. Make sure that:

- you read using daylight, whenever possible
- if you use electric lighting, it is neither too bright nor dull
- the ambient temperature is about 20 degrees Celsius
- you adopt a posture that puts minimum strain on muscles
- the chair supports your legs.

Finally, if you wish to improve your concentration in general, here are two exercises that you can practise at any time during the day.

■ Look outside your window and focus on what is there. If you can, say aloud what you see. Give a judgement about the shapes or the colours; be precise and use adjectives to qualify the images. For example. 'the greyish clouds seem to be in a hurry; the red car parked at the kerb could do with a wash; the grass looks freshly cut.' Make it last two minutes. Go back to your desk and try to recall what you saw.

■ Take a watch with a second hand. It completes its cycle in sixty seconds. This exercise has three degrees of difficulty. First, watch the hand as it begins a new cycle and don't let your eyes wander from the moving hand. When you can watch one whole revolution without distraction you have overcome the first difficulty. Now, keep the focus as before, and at the same time count in your mind backwards from ten to one slowly so that you finish with one when the second hand completes its cycle. Do this several times, until it becomes less difficult. Finally, continue to watch the second hand while counting in your mind and repeat a nursery rhyme, or a piece of verse. How are you getting on? You may have to persevere...

## Reduce the effects of dyslexia

Most poor readers have nothing intrinsically wrong. They simply find acquiring reading skills more difficult than learning, say, arithmetic or computer languages or music. However, some poor readers have an emotional or medical reason for their learning difficulty with reading. Dyslexia simply means the learning difficulty caused by a medical problem. The term 'learning difficulties' covers symptoms caused by emotional or linguistic problems and a variety of medical causes. 'Specific developmental dyslexia' is used when the problem can be medically categorised, and it is usually diagnosed in childhood due to the obvious symptoms (see McAuslan (6)).

Much progress has been made in the past few years towards an understanding of what dyslexia is, but there is an enormous amount still to be learned and understood. Dyslexia can vary from a very mild childhood form to one which continues to cause substantial difficulties throughout life. Dyslexia may be a consequence of partial deafness when young, or be induced by emotional tension or some brain malfunction. It is unlikely that anyone with a substantial degree of dyslexia would be reading this book.

But what of the person who has not been diagnosed as having a learning difficulty or dyslexia, but who privately has to struggle hard to keep up with his or her contemporaries? First there is the obvious evidence of difficulty in learning. reading skills. Then there might be more specific symptoms of dyslexia including an inability to distinguish left from right, or confusing objects with their mirror images. This is called 'crossed laterality'. It is manifest, for example, in confusing 'b' with 'd', or confusing the spelling of 'from' and 'form'. People with severe dyslexia may read 'puppy' as 'small dog', or 'Belgium' as 'Holland' (see Anthony Smith (7)). The characteristics common to these pairs of words indicate that the brain makes many correct associations, but fails to select the single correct word at the end of the reading/visualising/recall process.

It is best for someone with a significant learning difficulty to seek professional help. But if you suspect you may have a mild form, you can help yourself to read faster by using a multi-sensory approach. You need to learn to read using, simultaneously, as many of your senses as possible. You acquire such a capability by drill. For example, here are three very simple practices.

- The use of a guide - the finger as a pointer run vertically down the centre of the page at a reasonably fast speed - is one. The eyes are forced to follow the guide. This improves reading discipline and speed. (See Chapter 7 for details of 'pacers' to gain reading speed.)

- Moderately dyslexic people sometimes have erratic eye movements. A very simple visual aid, to train the eye to move horizontally, may correct this problem. The aid is a window or slot cut in the centre of a large postcard. The window is in the shape and size of one line of print. As the window is run down the page, the eye is limited to horizontal movements since the window shows only one line at a time.

- Place a pink transparent plastic sheet over the page you wish to read. The physical aspect of reading will be greatly eased.

Sensory assistance can help your reading in other ways. Link the words read (or groups of words) to as many sensory impressions as possible. Groups of words can be hooked on to images (little scenes described by the text) or your knowledge of the light, the sounds, the smell or touch of objects associated with the text you are reading. A young person may be helped if the observed scene is linked to reading. In the extreme, if a brown furry cat in the garden is crouching to catch a bird, the key words of the scene may be written down (possibly in brown ink), and by touching the cat (probably later) and smelling the garden (maybe the grass has been cut recently). In this way connections may be established between the words and other senses.

## Hands-on exercises

In this chapter there are exercises in the text. To be of long-term value, these exercises should be repeated regularly, once a day or once a week.

# 7

# Increase Your Reading Speed: the Dynamics of Reading

**PREPARE FOR READING**

**YOUR INITIAL READING SPEED**

**MOTIVATION**

**EYE MOVEMENTS AND REGRESSION**

**PERIPHERAL VISION**

**USE A GUIDE**

**CONDITIONING - INTRODUCING RHYTHM**

**CONSOLIDATION**

**REST YOUR EYES**

**MAINTAIN YOUR SPEED**

**HANDS-ON EXERCISES**

## Prepare for reading

You must change your reading habits if you want to get through the bumf faster. This Chapter will show you how. Suspend judgement until you have given the techniques a fair trial. Offence against Bumf means that you will move your eyes differently; this will allow you to pick things up faster and reduce the time you spend reading bumf.

This chapter gives you the techniques to increase your visual skills and to improve the dynamics of your reading. To familiarise yourself with the material and to learn to anticipate, browse through this chapter looking at the sub-headings, the diagrams, the summary at the beginning and the recommended exercises at the end. To work through the chapter, doing the exercises with a cooperative friend, should take about one hour.

This skill makes the same demands upon the learner as acquiring any other new skill, say skiing. Be child-like in your attitude. Children quickly sense the exhilaration of other children who can already ski. Their sole objective is to be able to enjoy themselves in the same way. They learn quickly because that objective is always before them. They accept short-term setbacks, like falling over. Being child-like means being unafraid of making mistakes. That is learning: finding out what works and what does not work. Children do not question the instructions. Today, you are on the nursery slopes, with a limited speed and limited bumf-beating capability. No one will know of your mistakes as you learn to read rapidly. Look to the top of the mountain and be determined that you, too, will enjoy the thrill or speed.

Have a stopwatch or clock, a sheet of paper and a pencil by you. Use Table 7.1 or copy it on to the paper to record your progress. Ensure that your lighting is comfortable. Minimise the possible interruptions. Choose a comfortable chair and place it by a table. In some exercises below, it is best if you have the help of a friend.

Now, select a book. As we are going to learn a skill together, it is important that we choose a book that is interesting and light. Go for a novel, avoiding 'classics' or humorous books. You are going in the shallow end of the pool for a few exercises, before you plunge in the deep end. It is better to tackle the technique with something that is easy to understand rather than multiplying the difficulties by adding deep philosophy (for which you may wish to stop and think) or strong humour (which needs laughter time).

## Table 7.1 Results of Reading Exercises

| Exercise | Speed | Compre-hension |
|---|---|---|
| 1  Initial reading | | |
| 2  Motivation | | |
| 3  Overcoming regression | | |
| 4  Peripheral vision | | |
| 5  Using a guide | | |
| 6  Conditioning | | |
| 7  Consolidation | | |

New books, particularly paperbacks, should be 'broken in'. A book that wants to shut all the time is not helping you to read it. Place the book with its spine on the table. Open it at page 30. With the palm of your hand, press it hard open. Move your palm up and down the pages, against the spine so that the book stays open at that page. Repeat this process every 30 pages or so to the end of the book. Do not open the book in the middle, bending the covers backwards to meet: it breaks the spine of the book and the pages will fall out soon.

We will now proceed step-by-step, with a series of exercises to illustrate and practise each step. The overall objective is to make you a faster reader by improving your existing visual skills. That will mean building on what you already know, and perhaps changing one or two of your past habits. Now, think positively - you can read faster.

# Your initial reading speed

### Reading instructions
Set yourself a reading time: two, three or five minutes and set your watch. Start reading the book, as you do normally. When the time is

up, make a mark with your pencil where you stopped and calculate your speed, using the formula given in Chapter 6. Record your speed on Table 7.1. Also give yourself a mark between 0 and 10 to express your comprehension. This mark must reflect what you think you got from the reading. Do you have a good, general idea of what you read? Did you miss some bits or have you forgotten them already? Is it important? Can you go on? Evaluating comprehension each time you do a reading exercise will give you a rough idea of your reading progress. We will work on comprehension in more detail later.

The reading speed for the average English-speaking person is between 200 and 300 words per minute. If you are slightly below, let's say you are within the range. If you are above, you have a head-start. If you are very much below, you will have to pay attention to your faults and practise to correct them.

So, we are equipped with an initial or reference speed which we are going to improve.

# Motivation

### Reading instructions

Your objective now is to double your reading speed. Whatever you achieved in the first exercise, aim to double it. To encourage you to do this, let's play a game. Suppose that if you double your speed you will win a superb prize.

Now, take the book again, and start reading from the last pencil mark. Read for the same amount of time as you did for Exercise 1. Mark the book with the pencil where you stopped. Note your speed and comprehension at Exercise 2.

You have achieved a higher speed than before or, indeed, you have doubled your speed. You have experienced motivation. You may be surprised that it was not very difficult. Motivation is the basic step that you have to apply every time you pick up something to read. But sometimes people feel rushed and fear they are missing something. To overcome this problem you need to:

- establish objectives or clarify your reading objectives
- read in short bursts.

Before you proceed with other exercises, it will help you if you set an objective now. In the novel that you have started, are you going to follow the plot or the main character? You may be uncertain which to choose. Here are a few guidelines to help you.

☑ If you are reading an adventure book with much action but characters are described simply and they do not change psychologically during the book, choose the plot.

☑ If you are reading a story that evolves around people who are described in depth, perhaps one person emerges as a key character, at least for the moment: if it is likely that this character will change behaviour as the story unfolds, choose this character (even if you have to change character as you get deeper into the novel).

☑ Do not choose both a character and the plot.

☑ You may think there is a lot more in this book, style, atmosphere - yes there may be, but right now, ignore it. We will talk about that later in this chapter.

Setting objectives is essential for comprehension, and will make working on your visual skills easier. So before you read further, say 'My objective is to follow the plot', or whatever you decide.

## Eye movements and regression

Ask a friend to sit opposite you about one metre away. Hold your book up, so that he or she can see your eye movements over the book, while you read two or three lines. Ask your friend to describe the eye movements that he or she saw. View similarly the eye movements of your friend when she or he reads. Your descriptions will probably follow Figure 7.1.

The aim of this exercise is to observe the number of stops the eyeballs make per line. You need to be particularly observant here so that you can say to your friend 'Your eyes stopped four times, or six times per line.' It is not good enough to say 'Your eyes moved from left to right.'

In the figure, each balloon represents the eye resting on a word or group of words. In Figure 7.1 the eye goes forward five times, skips backward three spaces, then goes forward four more times.

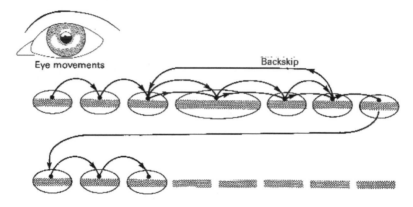

*Figure 7.1 - Untrained Eye Movements*

That is, eyes move with jerky movements or saccades, as these were first named. They take in a word or group of words and recognise the shape of the letters; the brain recalls the meaning of the word or words, then the eyes go on to the next word or group of words, and then to the next, and at each group the eye-brain process takes place. Now, the eyes may *go back* to check what was read before - perhaps because it is a foreign name or because the word is unfamiliar. Then the process starts again, until the eyes reach the end of the line and then ... zoom ... like an old-fashioned typewriter carriage, the eye starts again on the next line.

Every time the eyes stop on a word, it is called a fixation. Untrained eyes will fixate six to eight times per line. Every time the eyes go back to check on a word, it is called regression or backskipping.

A fixation can last from a split second to one second in very slow readers. One of the first things that you must try to do is to reduce the number of fixations to, say, three per line. And the first principle you are to put into practice is to eliminate regression. This will help you to read smoothly. The smoother your eye movements, the faster you read. Can you also be aware of a sense of rhythm.

Why do you regress? Because you are unsure of what you read and think that you have missed something important. That may be true, but it is inefficient. There are two possibilities: either it is important and the author will mention that word again, or it is not, so why worry about it?

As you go on and pick up speed, avoiding regression will become easier: the speed will make you concentrate more. This in turn will heighten your overall comprehension and will encourage you to anticipate. Regression will become redundant.

### Reading instructions

Now pick up your book and read for the same amount of time as you did before. Your aim is to go faster than last time. You will achieve this by reducing the number of fixations per line and by avoiding regression. Mark your book with a pencil where you have stopped. Calculate your speed, and record speed and comprehension against Exercise 3. This should not be difficult to achieve, and as you become more familiar with the names, regression is unnecessary.

# Peripheral vision

Sit opposite a friend, about a metre apart. Have your friend hold his or her index fingers, tip touching each other, between your faces, at the distance from you where you normally hold a book. Your friend will now move his or her fingers apart, horizontally, slowly. You must look at his or her eyes, not fingers. When one of the fingers goes out of your field of vision tell him or her to stop moving it. Do the same on the other side. Now look at the space between the two fingers. Repeat the exercise with the fingers moving vertically. See Figure 7.2.

You can determine your peripheral vision by yourself if you stare at one letter in a line of print. Place a finger on the letters each side of it. Then move the fingers apart until you can no longer recognise the recently uncovered letters. The distance between the fingers is probably wider than you expected. It represents your peripheral vision. You should be able to see and understand five average words in a group.

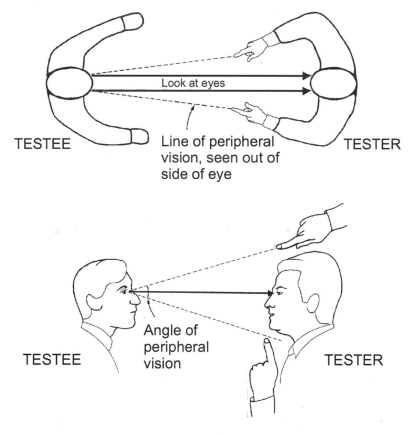

*Figure 7.2 - Peripheral Vision Assessment*
*(by permission of Tony Buzan)*

You use peripheral vision every day - when you drive, for instance. Without moving your eyes, you notice that a traffic light is changing colour, a child is about to run across the road, and so on. All the while you are concentrating and looking straight ahead.

When it comes to reading, however, you make little use of this peripheral vision if you look at only one word at a time. Focus your eyes on a particular word in a line of print, then try to read the words on either side. With training you can 'take in' several words at a time (in one fixation) so that you now read as shown in Figure 7.3. Note that the eye focuses on larger groups of letters or words than before. The eye goes to the centre of each balloon and uses peripheral vision to see the characters which fill the distance between the centre and the edge of each balloon. Thus a few centimetres at each end of the line are read by using peripheral vision, and now the eye is moving a shorter distance from left to right than it was before.

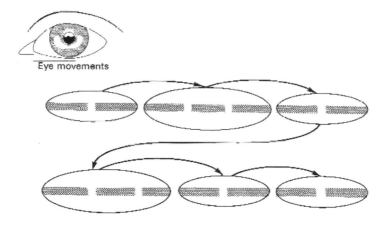

*Figure 7.3 - Eye Movements Using Peripheral Vision*

As peripheral vision is so useful it is worth exercising to improve it. Draw a vertical line down the middle of a page of text. Then focusing only on the vertical line, at the first line of text, see how many letters are seen to either side of the vertical line. Move down the vertical, and the number of letters seen by the peripheral vision will increase with practice.

| | |
|---:|:---|
| a | c |
| wy | zo |
| nip | zag |
| ads | uvwy |
| and so | on and |

If you don't make peripheral vision work for you, you waste a lot of effort and energy reading blank margins, at both ends of each line!

### Reading instructions

Now take your book again, at the last pencil mark, and start reading. Remember to follow plot or character, to take in larger groups of words in one fixation, and to read faster than before. You will achieve this by starting to read two or three words into the line and stopping two or three words before the end of each line. Read for the same time as before.

When you have finished this reading exercise, mark the book with a pencil to note where you stopped, calculate and record your speed at Exercise 4. Your speed may have gone down. There is no cause for alarm. This is a learning process, and learning is made of highs and lows. Just remember the first time you climbed on to a bicycle: you probably concentrated on watching the front wheel and kept falling off until, as if by magic, it all came together - posture, movement, looking up straight, and you were speeding down the road, probably unable to stop and get off safely.

# Use a guide

Sit opposite your friend again, and ask him or her to draw a circle in the air with his or her eyes, i.e. follow the circumference of an imaginary circle which may be around your head. Observe the eye movements and describe what you see. Probably the eyes moved following a shape like that shown in Figure 7.4.

Now, guide your friend's eyes with your finger, by drawing an imaginary circle in the air. Your friend's eyes follow the finger. Observe your friend's eyes again. Their movement now is smoother, like that shown in Figure 7.5.

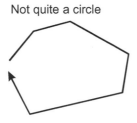

Not quite a circle                    More like a circle

*Figure 7.4 - Unguided eye*          *Figure 7.5 - Guided eye*
*movements*                            *movements*

This suggests that to help your eyes move smoothly on a page, and to avoid wandering off and regressing, you need to guide your eyes when you read. Initially, the guide will take your eyes along each line, and down the page, line by line. This is something that you already do. If you are suffering from toothache you take the telephone book to look for the telephone number of your dentist. You use your finger to search down the column for the correct name and number. Why? Because you are in pain and are trying to save time as well as not wishing to make an incorrect call. You are motivated

So, from now on, use a finger or the tip of a pencil as a guide - whichever feels comfortable when you read. A finger is recommended because usually you have it with you and thus you have no excuse for not using it while reading!

*Figure 7.6 - Using a finger as a reading guide or pacer*

## Reading instructions

Let us put this into practice. Take your book again and start reading, for the same amount of time as before, starting at your last pencil mark. Remember to apply *motivation*, that is to read faster than before, to follow your objective, to *avoid regression*, and to *group the words* - fixating, say, twice or less per line, to avoid reading from margin to margin. Use your finger while you read for this exercise (Figure 7.6).

Mark your book where you have stopped, calculate your speed and record both speed and comprehension at Exercise 5 - Using a guide.

The result here may come as an agreeable surprise: your speed - and even your comprehension- went up. But if you think the finger or pencil slowed you down, then move it faster!

You may also have found the guide a distraction, or that using it felt strange. Don't give up: persevere. You are not used to using a guide systematically, as you have just done. With practice, the guide will help you to gather speed and will focus your concentration.

## Can you swim or do you run?

An analogy may persuade you. Imagine that you have joined a swimming or running club and that you practise once or twice a week with your fellow members. In swimming, people practise in lanes, depending on their speed. Very quickly, you know which person you like to follow and which other person you do not like to follow. Those swimming too slowly are infuriating because you keep catching them up. It destroys your sense of rhythm. Those swimming too fast exhaust you. You need to put in too much effort to keep the same distance and your rhythm is also upset. Similarly runners have pacers to follow.

In reading, the guide is the ideal person in front of you: it is slightly ahead of where you are reading; it prompts you to go faster, it allows you to maintain a comfortable rhythm.

# Conditioning - introducing rhythm

Some people have an innate sense of rhythm and find it easy to apply. One way to start is to move along the lines following your heartbeats, so that your finger (or pencil) traces one line per heartbeat. Do this for a page or two.

Now try to increase the pace either by saying line, line, line to yourself, or by using a metronome set at a speed slightly faster than is comfortable. Do this for two pages, or until it feels natural.

We are now going to practise high-speed reading with rhythm. You are going to read from your last pencil mark, using a guide and rhythm. Start at a comfortable pace and then progressively speed up until you cannot move your guide fast enough to keep up with the rhythm. At this point you will have to zig-zag down the page tracing a maximum of three zig-zags per page (see Figure 7.7).

*Figure 7.7 - Fast Reading Conditioning with Rhythm*

To practise conditioning correctly, you need to hold your book correctly, with your left hand at the top of the right-hand page to turn the pages, while your right hand does the zig-zag movements, if you are right handed. If you are left handed and using your left hand as your reading guide, turn the pages with your right hand, so that the rhythm is maintained.

Set your watch for five minutes now and start from the last pencil mark. Remember that you are constantly speeding up, moving down the pages very fast to end up at the rate of about one page per second. You may experience a blur during the exercise. This is normal. Your eyes need to adjust to this new way of receiving and sending the information to the brain. To keep your motivation, start to look for keywords or each page. If you take in half a dozen words you are doing very well. Start now, and get hooked on speed!

### Reading instructions
We are not going to record this speed - it was a practice exercise. Go back to your last pencil mark, the one you made at the end of Exercise

5. Set your watch for slightly longer than before and start reading, using all the techniques you have learned so far. Read, going as fast: as you can with some comprehension.

When the time is up, mark your book where you have stopped, calculate your speed and record it under Exercise 6, Conditioning, on Table 7.1. It is a fair bet that you have exceeded your own expectations. Your reading speed is a lot higher. Why? Because shortly before you read, you were conditioned to read faster.

Like an athlete before a competition, you have warmed up your muscles to be ready for use when you need them. The rhythm became natural and your eyes got used to moving rapidly, following your guide. Although you read more slowly in this last recorded exercise, you were influenced by the high-speed conditioning. We are similarly influenced by speed when we drive on a motorway at a constant 70 miles per hour for a long time. When we want to take the sliproad marked clearly at 40 mph, we rarely slow to this: we brake a little, convinced that we are doing the required speed. The actual speed is probably more like 50 mph and that seems very slow!

If your reading speed is considerably improved, well done! Now, let us look into comprehension more carefully: we must bring speed and comprehension into unison.

If your comprehension is adequate, skip the next few lines and go on to the next exercise. If your comprehension is low, let us check a few things:

? Are you clear about your objective, what are you following - plot or character?
? Do you keep this in mind while you read?
? Do you move your guide smoothly underneath the lines of your page?
? Do you look for keywords along each line?

If you answer 'yes' to all these, then slow down. At this stage, there is no point in having speed for speed's sake.

If your answer is 'no', then pinpoint where you are going wrong and alter your habits. Then repeat the last exercise.

The speed used in the conditioning exercise is the speed you will apply when you overview a document quickly; this is described in Chapter 8. It is important that you understand the value of conditioning, practising zig-zagging to enhance your concentration and speed. Once you have experienced this several times, it becomes a habit and a necessary step to recognising quickly what you need in a document. It is only when you have mastered conditioning that you can claim to read faster and with flexibility - high speed in order to overview, and a more leisurely speed - a cruising speed - to read what really interests you.

# Consolidation

### Reading instructions

Take your book and begin to read from the last pencil mark. Read to consolidate everything we have learned so far. We are now trying to bring speed and comprehension together. Relax. Do not worry about technique: you have mastered it. Enjoy your book. Probably you will need to slow down. Do so. Aim to double your initial speed, with a comprehension estimate of 7 or 8. To achieve this, be flexible when you read: you now have a range of speeds to choose from. Use them. When the story interests you (it depends on your objective), slow down. When it does not, or it is repetitive, speed up. Do not skip - that is not reading - but get a general idea, perhaps using your highest speed.

## How do you drive a car?

Suppose you want to drive to Scotland from the South of England. Your aim is to get there quickly. The motorway is the obvious route. Almost always in top gear, you get there quickly.

Once arrived, one morning you wish to explore the area. You take the scenic route and admire the countryside, using the gear lever frequently around the bends, avoiding sheep, in second or third gear. You enjoy the ride. Later that day you make your way back to the hotel via a straight rapid road. You have used the gears and speeds of your car to fulfil your needs.

Like driving a car, the speeds that you have mastered with your novel are now ready to be used. Your final overall speed will be an average. Vary your speed according to what is in front of you. Do not become the prisoner of one speed. Read for at least five minutes. When this time is up, mark your book where you have stopped, calculate your speed and record it under Exercise 7, Consolidation. You have probably doubled your reading speed. With practice you could triple it. Your comprehension is high, about 8 out of 10. A great feeling of achievement.

Your reading should be more stable now. You have motivation, you have an objective, you are eliminating regression, you are grouping the words, you are using a guide to help you focus and concentrate, you can speed up.

If you are still having difficulties, which is not uncommon at this stage, repeat exercises where you find difficulty. Learning a skill is unpredictable: some wonder why they did not take it up sooner, others stumble here or there and take a little longer. Remember you only started to read faster an hour or two ago. All this is new and you are changing some habits that have been with you for many years.

## Rest your eyes

You may have found these exercises tiring for your eyes or you may experience tired eyes without trying to read faster. Here are two exercises to rest your eyes.

- Put your elbows on a table. Shape your hands into small cups in which you are going to rest your eyes. The word 'rest' is important. Do not apply pressure to the eyeballs as this would make the exercise useless. You should feel comfortable.

  Close your eyes and create a picture. Imagine that you are standing in a large golden-yellow cornfield. It is a sunny summer day. Look all around you. Look to the left. There is a tall poplar rising to the sky. Look at it from the trunk up; look at the green leaves against the blue sky. In the sky, on the right, there is a plane cruising from the right to the left. Now look at your feet: there are poppies, bright red poppies and in the distance, far away, on the right there is a church spire that rises on the horizon. Look at the whole scene again: the golden-yellow corn, the tall green tree, the blue sky and the plane moving from right to left, the red poppies at your feet and the church spire in the distance. Remember that all this should be done without feeling any pressure on your eyes.

  When you take your hands away and open your eyes, things around you are much brighter and your eyes feel refreshed.

- Another simple exercise is to focus on a far point - ideally out of a window. Hold the position for five seconds and then, without moving your head, focus on the nearest point in the room and maintain your focus for two or three seconds. Repeat the exercise five times.

Both these exercises require that you move the muscles that surround your eyes. You move them sideways and up and down. It helps to keep your eyes in good shape. Visualising colour in the dark also has a restful effect. These exercises do not take long and are particularly beneficial if you work in artificial light (see WH Bates (10).

# Maintain your speed

When you feel that you have mastered the technique of reading faster while maintaining comprehension (and it may take a little longer than doing the seven exercises), how do you keep your new skill?

You will need to practise about five minutes every day. One recalls here the words of a ballerina: *'If you do not practise one day, you notice it. If you don't practise for two days, the public notices it!'* The practice takes the form of high-speed conditioning. The best material to practise on is a newspaper, because it has narrower columns and therefore you need only one fixation per line. Also, as a rule, a newspaper article, such as a leader, summarises a situation with which you are already familiar. It is easy to read quickly, until you come to new information or opinion, at which point you will slow down, but still keep a fast rhythm.

You may be wondering how fast you should read? There is no limit. What you feel is comfortable becomes the norm.

Remember that flexibility is synonymous with rapid reading, and that to get at what you want quickly is as important as reading and absorbing the information.

If you wish to go faster still, start the process again, in a step-by-step manner, as we have done through this chapter, focusing on speed first and comprehension later.

But, I hear you say, there is more to my book than the plot or character. In this case adopt the 'Book Reviewer Technique'. Many reviewers first read a book at a speed of 600 to 800 words per minute to see what the book is about. Once they know, they will read the book again, this time concentrating on, say, the credibility of characters, at the same speed. Now, if the book is well written, they will read the book again at that speed but looking at the English and enjoying it.

In other words, read the book with only one purpose in mind. If the book is worth it, it is better to read it two or three times at a good speed than once slowly, trying to follow everything at the same time.

## Hands-on exercises

 To practise getting information fast, look at a poster or a notice on a notice board for only three seconds, then look away and ask yourself:

- was this pleasant to read or easy to grasp?

- what was the document colour and typeface?

- could I describe the picture (trees or three paragraphs)?

- could I give details about the picture (trees were tall and thin, the sky had clouds on the right, or the typeface was small and one heading had an exclamation mark)?

 Look back at the picture or notice to check what you had learned from your quick glance and what you had missed. With practice you will learn more and more from similar quick glances.

 Practise conditioning reading a newspaper. The narrow columns make it easy for the eyes to speed down them. Give yourself a time limit. Check your speed.

# 8

# Increase Comprehension and Retention - A Systematic Approach to Complex Documents

---

**TREAT A BOOK AS A WHOLE**

**THE SIX STEPS TO SYSTEMATIC READING**

**WHY WAIT UNTIL THE END TO MAKE NOTES?**

**FLEXIBILITY IN READING**

**A TYPICAL DAY AND THE SIX-STEP APPROACH**

**HANDS-ON EXERCISES**

---

## Treat the book as a whole

Take a look at Figure 8.1. The dots perhaps have no meaning for you.

*Figure 8.1 What Pattern Fits This Picture?*

Once you know that a dalmatian dog is in the picture, you are able to find it, since we all have a mental pattern of a dalmatian dog.

Books have patterns too. The pattern is obvious in fiction, where a story-line is built around a hero and you follow him or her through various exploits and sub-plots. This concept of pattern is what is meant by 'wholeness'. The author had a plan and your first task for any reading material - a book, a report, an editorial or newspaper article - is to discover the author's plan. Rapid reading of a book requires you to refer to and consider the material as a whole, to consider that book's plan - and you must know that plan!

## The six steps to systematic reading

You have a book to read. These six steps are the systematic approach to reading a book.

## 1. Recap - brushing up your mind

### Purpose
This is a warm-up exercise, similar to that carried out by an athlete before a competition. It also helps the reader start to identify gaps in his or her knowledge.

### Method
Consider the title and jot down a few keywords describing what you know about the subject. This memory search puts you in a positive mode and prepares you to connect new information to the knowledge you already possess. People sometimes say that they know nothing about a subject. This is rarely true. Because of the quantity of information people are bombarded with through the media, through travel, through conversation, is there anything so utterly new that one's mind is an absolute blank? Remember what was said in Chapter 1: *'Reading faster is first an attitude'*. This positive attitude starts here. We gain motivation.

### Timing
This step should be done quickly, spending no more than two minutes.

## 2. Set objectives

### Purpose
An analysis of your objectives increases your concentration and helps you to achieve them. It also boosts your confidence and helps you to speed up.

### Method
This most important step applies to all reading material. What are you reading it for? This seems obvious. Yet those who complain that: they do not 'get on' with reading, or that they have to read every word, or that they get bored, do so because they did not spend a few minutes establishing their personal objectives. It is the comer-stone that makes your reading more efficient and memorable.

*113*

*'A man without a goal is like shooting a gun without a target.'*
Benjamin Franklin

If you don't know what you are looking for, how can you find it? A book, particularly a textbook, contains a lot of information. It caters for a variety of people and the author does not know who the reader may be. So the author develops some basic ideas, and links these to more sophisticated ones. It is the reader's job to choose what he or she needs and to concentrate on those parts, leaving the rest aside. When you establish your objectives, trust your own existing knowledge and feel confident.

How do you set objectives? By formulating one, two or three questions. Questions force you to look for answers and help you to keep focused. For example, when you began to read this book, the questions you asked yourself might have been:

**?** Will this book help me to read long office reports rapidly?(See this chapter.)
**?** Will I be able to read fiction twice as fast? (See Chapter 7.)
**?** Will I be able to escape from electronic bumf (See Chapter 2)

Again, you must ask yourself what you want. Do you want to improve your reading or information absorption ability? Is it familiarisation with the subject, deep understanding of the ideas, or reinforcement of your knowledge that you seek?

**Bad Objectives**
'If you do not know what question to ask, you do not comprehend what you are doing.' writes Frank Smith in his book *Reading* (3). Be specific when you set out your questions. Avoid all-embracing phrases such as 'get an awareness of' or 'acquire knowledge about', which is a common mistake among poorly motivated readers. Focus each question on a clear topic.

Sometimes people confuse Reading Objectives with Thinking Objectives. For example a reader may ask:

**?** 'Will this help my research?'
**?** 'Do the recommendations apply to us?'
**?** 'What do I need to do?'

These are *Thinking Objectives.* Readers can decide whether the material will help (or that it applies to them, or that they had to do this or that) only after they have absorbed what the document is about. The purpose of efficient reading is to get through documents faster so that you have more time to THINK about the information you have absorbed. It is not to read more.

Well-formulated objectives, combined with good visual skills, will give you more time for more important things than reading.

### Making the Pips Squeak
Why not give yourself a time limit as well? For example:

**?** 'Can I, in 10 minutes, familiarise myself with x, y and z?'
**?** 'Can I, in 30 minutes, outline X's arguments on Y?'
**?** 'Can I, in 20 minutes, summarise the Board's recommendations about the new computer system?'

Giving yourself a time limit allows you to measure your progress, keep an awareness of time and a concentrated mind.

### Timing
Don't set yourself unreasonable tasks. No more than five minutes.

## 3. Overview

### Purpose
This gives you the feel of the book. You start to locate the information you seek and you decide whether the book is worth reading.

### Method
Using the high-speed conditioning learned in Chapter 7, do an overview of the whole book. Pay attention to whatever stands out.

This will include the cover, the table of contents, the index, the introduction, the summaries, the tables, diagrams, illustrations, chapter headings and bullets (●) it contains. Flick through it very rapidly. This is not reading in the ordinary sense but looking at the structure, presentation and contents of the book. This is scanning a document, literally looking at the whole. If you can, make a mental note of where what you want (your objectives) is located in the book.

### Timing
Take five minutes for this exercise, literally flicking through the pages.

## 4. Preview

### Purpose
Preview keeps you focused. It is the art of rejection and keeps you from becoming sidetracked and distracted by irrelevant information (bumf).

### Method
Strike out, using a pencil, those parts of the document that do not meet your objectives. This also means rejecting bumf: repetition, padding or information that is already familiar. A glance, looking roughly four lines at a time, tells you whether a paragraph, a page or even a whole section contains the information you are seeking. It is not easy to do, as we are reluctant actively to discard what someone has written. But it is essential if you are to keep to your objectives. When you hesitate, look again at the objectives. Be ruthless in eliminating whatever is not relevant. When your objectives are well defined, it is easy - with practice, it comes naturally. This is skimming - reading superficially.

### Timing
Again, read as quickly as you can. The time will vary with the type of material, the way it is presented and according to how well you defined your objectives. A time for a typical book might be ten minutes.

## 5. Inview

### Purpose
Inview provides you with detailed understanding.

### Method
You have identified the points that interest you. You are focused and ready to read in depth. Read with comprehension in mind. Read line by line. If you have problems with comprehension, keep going: the answer may be on the next page. Continue to treat the material as a whole, building up knowledge as you read.

Your speed will depend on the nature of the book. It is important to keep a flexible approach. Use a pencil or highlighter to mark key ideas or key words. Now is the time to apply the rhythm and cruising speed we learned in Chapter 7. Try to keep a good speed, a 'tempo', where you are moving along comfortably, but under slight pressure.

If at the end of this in-depth reading you have gaps in your comprehension, read the book again. It is surprising how much better comprehension and retention are if you read, rapidly, the same material two or three times rather than slogging through once, stopping at every difficulty. So, when you have a problem, make a mental note or mark the page and continue. Return to the problem later, if necessary.

### Timing
Set yourself a realistic time for this task and stick to it. In Steps 1 to 4 you cut out lots of unnecessary reading. Now you can be generous (20-30 minutes) to ensure you achieve your objectives.

## 6. Review

### Purpose
To check that all objectives are met and to reinforce retention.

### Method
To consolidate what you have read, you must link it to your previous

knowledge. Make a Mind Map®. This enhances long-term memory because you hook new information on to what you already know. It is also early use of this new material which means that it will become part of your knowledge. Review is also a way to check whether any fuzzy areas remain which you may need to go back to briefly later. The Mind Map® is the way to summarise and link ideas. Do it from memory. If you have information gaps, refer to your document and fill in these gaps with a different colour.

### Timing
Depending on the amount of detail, a typical time for one book may be ten minutes, but you may need longer.

## Why wait until the end to make notes?

Make notes at the end of all the reading steps. This makes you selective about the information you choose to keep. Do not make notes from the text as you read. These notes will reflect the sequence of ideas as you read them. It is inefficient because:

- It is time consuming.
- The notes will be unnecessarily bulky.
- It encourages mental laziness.
- It does not indicate that you are absorbing what you read.
- The notes may not be necessary.

Notes made after all the different reading steps contain what the document means to you. It is now part of your mental property or knowledge. To ensure long-term retention of it, you need to link it to what was already in your memory. In order to do this, you will probably use a different layout or sequence from that used in the book because the information is yours and fits into your experience.

Also, writing and reading are two different activities, requiring different mental and physical actions. When they are mixed, each interrupts the other as you go back and forth between them and this disturbs your reading rhythm. When they are separated, they reinforce each other.

Now, if we apply this idea to the passage we read from *The Pickwick Papers*, we can summarise it as shown in Figure 8.2. The Mind Map® is made around the three main subjects. Unfortunately they do not evoke the atmosphere presented by Dickens' prose. Thus it is important to highlight and remember that Mind Maps® do not replace linear writing! However, from these notes you could easily tell a friend - or an audience - about the passage. The asterisks (*) show the links between subjects.

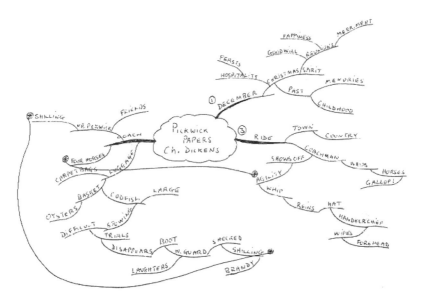

*Figure 8.2 - Mind Map®: Pickwick Papers*

## Flexibility in reading

Although we have been through a systematic approach to the reading of books, there are differences between individuals and between the documents they handle. Some steps can be omitted. We are going to have a look at specialised reports and put this to the test in the next chapter.

Learning to read faster is like learning to cook. First you learn the rules. You must acquire some basic principles like how to cook green vegetables or red meats; then you refine this knowledge with the elements for simple sauces. Once you have got the basics, and understand why things are done this way, you can adapt any recipe to your own taste, what feels right for you. So you must follow the rules until they become second nature. When that stage is reached, you can skip a stage, or combine two, just as you would with your favourite dishes - add more salt or substitute for the cream to suit your needs and the ingredients that are available.

**Above all, be flexible.**

# A typical day and the six-step approach

At this stage we need to consider your typical day in the office. How can the 6-step approach be used?

### The twice-a-day, once-a-week and twice-a-year principle
First, as the post is distributed **each morning**, sort it in piles.

- Pile I contains letters, memos and emails which require immediate attention and action, or which can be answered - or delegated - right away, and do so. If there may be a delay and the incoming document may float around your desk for more than a day, then put it, together with any related notes or letters, in a transparent plastic folder. The folder acts as a reminder that it must be dealt with very soon.

- Pile 2 contains documents which require some time to be read, or documents which can only be dealt with after more information is assembled.

Second, set **a day in the week** in which you will do your serious reading (Pile 2), and makes this a routine. Ideally this is first thing in the morning, so that you benefit from natural lighting and a refreshed mind. A rule of thumb is to devote two hours per week. If possible, close the door, redirect the telephone, eliminate distractions and read uninterrupted, using the six-step approach.

Third, **twice a year**, go through your long-term filing system. Clipped articles, kept reports or booklets which are no longer accurate, nor relevant to your job are binned. Get rid of 70% of this material by throwing it away, passing it to colleagues to whom it may be useful, or send it back to the Central Filing system.

There may be a document that has to be read that day and between other tasks. So how do you proceed?

Say it is 9 o'clock and someone hands you a report saying that they would value your opinion on it. You have a meeting at 9:15 and thus cannot devote much time to it. If the topic is unfamiliar, or you find it hard to motivate yourself to read it, do a recap.

Then, establish your reading objectives, and go to the meeting.

Coming back just before lunch, take a few minutes to do an overview, familiarising yourself with the presentation of the document, checking if your objectives will be answered, or whether you should change these objectives now. Then put the report aside and go to lunch.

On your return, you expect a visitor. Proceed with a preview in as short a time as possible, before receiving your visitor. When the visitor leaves, immerse yourself in the report. Stop all distractions, read {inview) and review the report.

## Hands-on exercises

 **Take a document out of your in-tray. Flick through it. Be critical: can you tell what it is about? Can you find an Executive Summary or a Conclusion easily?**

☞ Put the six-step approach to work with one long (over 500 pages) document.

☞ Go through your long-term filing system. Can you discard at least 50% of it?

☞ If you receive a document and you have no clear idea why, or you have difficulty in forming an objective to read it, ask 'Why has the sender sent it to me?' Be critical; do you need to read it at all?

☞ Practise recall patterns immediately after a meeting. Have you missed anything of importance? If you have, why?

# 9

# Apply the Six Steps to Reading Articles

> **A FINANCIAL TIMES ARTICLE**
>
> **A PIECE FROM A BOOK**

## A Financial Times article

The article in Figure 9.1 is taken From *The Financial Times* (August 17, 2004). Suppose you are interested in it and decide to apply your newly learned technique. Generally, newspapers, journals and magazines lack space which results in well-edited pieces. The fluff or irrelevances - bumf - have been taken out. You can, therefore, combine Step 3 (Preview) and 4 (Inview). As you are interested in current affairs, you may feel that a Recap (Step 1) with a newspaper article is usually unnecessary.

Have you ever tried to write an article for publication? You are usually given a maximum number of words to write. You find it difficult to confine yourself to this limitation and send off your draft. The editor will send it back to you suggesting, amongst other things, that you drop this and that paragraph. You are aghast, thinking 'they' are pruning out your best bits! Trust them. The editor's experience is making your article more focused and easier for the reader to grasp your thinking. Consider the article overleaf.

Tuesday August 17 2004

# The empire moves its frontiers

## US troop withdrawals herald a moment of history

With the US administration's tendency towards high-flown terminology about 'military transformation' and the 'usability of forces', it is easy to miss the historic import of yesterday's announcement by President George W. Bush that the US will reduce its troop presence in bases overseas by 70,000 soldiers - about one third - by the end of the decade.

To be sure, it is hard to argue with the logic of the move, particularly in Europe, where America and its Nato allies have not faced a threat from across the Fulda Gap for almost a generation. Without Soviet tanks to repel, it makes little sense to keep two of the US army's 10 armoured divisions stationed in the Bavarian forests. Yet the decision marks the end of an era in which the world's most war-torn continent was finally pacified with the help of a benign foreign army.

Rarely has a foreign power remained in such numbers over such a long period and then withdrawn with local inhabitants expressing sorrow rather than anger.

Emperor Honorius's decision to withdraw his Roman legions from Britain in 410 AD, despite the pleadings of local Britons besieged

**The US is stepping up its departure from Europe at a time when Nato, its most important international military alliance, is still grappling for a purpose**

by invading Picts and Saxons, is a distinctly dim historical memory.

Equally important, the Americans withdraw, unlike Honorius, having successfully completed their mission. The Soviet threat has disappeared. Nor is there any danger that a newly unified and industrialised Germany will resort to militaristic romanticism. In one of history's great ironies, Germany's one-time enemies now find themselves attempting (with some success) to prod the sleeping giant into more active military involvement in places such as Bosnia, Afghanistan and Iraq.

Bosnia, Afghanistan and Iraq.

Even in Asia, where US troop presence has been far more contentious, anti-American demonstrations have become an annual event in Seoul and Okinawa - there is obvious ambivalence about the prospect of a US withdrawal. Part of that schizophrenia has to do with the continuing security risks that exist in the region. North Korea possesses ballistic missiles that can reach Tokyo and more conventional ones that can reach Seoul. China continues to expand, its large battery of rockets aimed at Taipei. As recently as last month Beijing held war games that amounted to a very public mock invasion of Taiwan.

The world is torn between a suspicion of the solitary superpower, and a more general appreciation for Pax Americana. Older Koreans well remember the US-led United Nations forces that pushed back the invading North half a century ago. The extent of that nostalgia even today can perhaps best be seen in the Philippines, where an almost universal wish to see the US military leave has led to a ruefulness now that they are gone.

The very real achievements of US forces in Europe and Asia over the past 60 years should not obscure the problems they have left in their wake, however. The goodwill that once existed in Asia has increasingly dissipated across the continent, as younger Koreans and nationalist Japanese increasingly question the enduring US presence. The Bush administration's insistent sabre rattling towards Pyongyang in particular has severely damaged America's previous image of benign paternalism.

Similarly, the US is stepping up its departure from Europe at a time when Nato, its most important international military alliance, is still groping for a purpose. Donald Rumsfeld, US defence secretary, has repeatedly asserted his commitment to the alliance. Yet the US administration's desire to form 'coalitions of the willing' to pursue its policies, rather than depend on its old allies, has left deep wounds. Divisions over Iraq still sting and the inability of Nato's European members to find even the most basic equipment to expand the alliance's role in Afghanistan does not bode well for an organisation that has vowed to play a global security role.

The US withdrawal from Europe and Asia is not, like Britain's pull back from east of Suez in the 1960s, a retreat from empire. Whether it likes it or not, the US is creating an entirely new 'footprint' for its overseas presence. The 130,000 troops currently in Iraq are unlikely to be brought home soon, and the 18,000 in Afghanistan are similarly there for the foreseeable future. New bases are popping up in places such as Qatar and Djibouti, and more are expected to be established in Romania and Bulgaria.

That is why yesterday's announcement, while welcomed by most of the US military establishment, has a distinct feel of rearranging the deck chairs, rather than rethinking the destination. The real issue facing American troops today is that there are too few of them to perform the jobs demanded of them. Mr Rumsfeld has steadfastly refused to increase the size of the military even as its global commitments continue to grow. John Kerry, the Democratic presidential candidate, has vowed to add 40,000 soldiers, mostly to the army which has almost all its active brigades either in Iraq and Afghanistan, or in the process of preparing to deploy there. Even as he brings the boys home, Mr Rumsfeld would be wise to follow suit.

*Figure 9.1 - FT Article 'The Empire moves its Frontiers'*
Reproduced with permission from the *Financial Times*

## Step 1 - Recap

Having looked at the news section of the Financial Times, you select this article because the Future of the European and American Defence interest you. No more is needed, as it is short.

## Step 2 - Set objectives

Why do you want to read this article beyond general interest? Be precise and set yourself a time limit. For example, can you, in five minutes, identify the reasons for the withdrawal of US troops? And why is it so important?

## Step 3 - Overview

Take about one minutes to scan zig-zagging the whole article. To your surprise you note several historical references. The answers are not obviously laid out.

## Step 4 - Preview and Step 5 - Inview

Combine Previewing and Inviewing - in other words, take four lines at a time, zig-zagging through the paragraphs which do meet your objectives. Slow down to two fixations per line when the information answers your objectives. In this way, you will spends four minutes reading this article.

## Step 6 - Review

Such a short piece does not need notes. But as you turn away from the article, consolidate in your mind what answers you have gained.

The second and fourth paragraphs give the first reason - the collapse of the Soviet threat. The fifth paragraph names the anti-American feeling in Asia - and its ambivalence considering existing threats. The seventh paragraph cites President GW Bush's unpopular stance and in the final paragraph, we are told that the current administration will not increase the size of the military. So altogether there are four reasons. Why this is so important is less clear: probably because of the ambivalence and ambiguity of the withdrawal in some regions at a time when Nato is still uncertain of its role.

# A piece from a book

This example is taken from Professor Geoffrey Best's book *'Churchill - a Study in Greatness'*, published in 2001 (22). I have chosen Chapter 12, entitled 'Chartwell and Hitler'. The extract below shows Churchill in the 1930s, having returned to Parliament, settled in his home, Chartwell, and becoming increasingly aware of the threat of Hitler. The passage below is the beginning of the Chapter.

---

If his India campaign was what Churchill was best known for through the early 1930s, his campaign to arouse Parliament and people to the dangers of Hitler's Germany took over as the earlier campaign petered out. But his private life at the same time was very important to him. He was continuously busy as a writer and had to be so because it was his only source of serious income and therefore the necessary means of caring for his wife, his children and his home. This is a good place for standing back to look at Churchill in mid-career.

He was not yet the great man he would soon become. Everyone recognised that he was an important man and a most uncommon man, the most uncommon man to have attained a high political office apart from David Lloyd George, who was at least as uncommon and who had attained the highest office of all. Like Lloyd George, he had made many enemies on his way to the top and, like him again, he was regarded by sound party men and political moralists as untrustworthy, though in an entirely different way. Lloyd George could never be anything but a Liberal, Churchill had been Conservative, Liberal and Constitutionalist, and it was not clear what he might be in ten years' time.

He still held to the belief that he was destined to do great things for the nation he loved, but when, if or how he would ever be able to do them seemed doubtful even to him. War was what especially excited him and brought out what was most original and powerful within him.

Aware of the dangers of such a temperament, he was not the bad sort of man who would wish to start a war in order to shine in it, but his early scepticism about the Treaty of Versailles had been borne out by subsequent events, and by now, the early 1930s, he felt more and more sure that what was still universally known as the Great War would sooner or later become called the First World War. Recollection of his own experiences between 1914 and 1918 continued to pain him. At its beginning, he had been the only member of the Cabinet who was cheerful and optimistic. His career had then still been on the upward path and, if only the Dardanelles expedition had turned out better, it might have led even to his overtaking his political colleague, mentor and rival, David Lloyd George, to become the Prime Minister who led his people to victory.

His experiences in the Great War stayed with Churchill for the rest of his life. We have seen how badly he had been hit and hurt by the Dardanelles failure and how he had been unfairly made the scapegoat for it. For about two years, from the middle of 1915 to the middle of 1917, he toiled under this shadow and strove to rise from beneath it. Only through the last eighteen months of the war had he been once again in a seat of power. He had filled it creditably; but at the armistice he was just one of the many ministers of a broad coalition government, not one of its inner circle and certainly not its star. The ten years that followed had seen him back in the political front line and back on the Conservative side of it, but he did not think much of the party's leader, he was viewed as vulgar and untrustworthy by the respectable society of conventional Christian gentlemen who composed its parliamentary strength, and he was openly hostile to its main policies from the turn of the 1930s. Would he ever appear at the political top again? Churchill thought it doubtful, and so did everyone else.

In personal terms, he was now well into his fifties and had acquired a more impressive presence than when he was younger. His body was a bit bulkier, the rather large balding head on top of it less disproportionate than it once had been; his face was fatter, readily delivering the chubby, saucy looks which encouraged the impression that he was always good-humoured and nice to everybody. In fact, he was not always nice to everybody. He could put on a good show of benevolence in public, but the truth is that he didn't enjoy mixing with people he didn't already know and, unless embarking on a well-prepared for public occasion or in the House of Commons, he much preferred being in private with familiar faces around him. Without thinking about it, he had grown into the style of taking servants for granted. (Some biographers define this as typically aristocratic, but it was just as characteristic of the late-Victorian upper middle class.) He had and he would retain a way of looking at subordinates and inconsequential strangers described by them variously as staring, scowling or glowering; sometimes, if there was a group of them, facing them down one by one. He was bossy and demanding, good-humoured and genial so long as he wasn't thwarted. He couldn't cope without a manservant or valet and he was unselfconsciously accustomed to having himself fussed over and looked after, and to living well. 'Winston,' said his bosom friend F. E. Smith, 'is a man of simple tastes. He is always prepared to put up with the best of everything.' He took exercise as often as he could: a practised rider, he had gone on playing polo until at last giving it up in 1925; he would still go out with the hounds when at Blenheim or with rich friends on their estates, and he was a keen and good swimmer.

His lifestyle did not appear to be a healthy one, but appearances were deceptive. Clementine, herself relatively abstemious, worried about his love of whisky, brandy and champagne. On festive occasions and in tense times, he drank more copiously than on working days, and it is impossible not to believe that some of the people who said they had witnessed him drinking too much had really done so, but overall there was justice in his remark, later in life, that he had taken more out of alcohol than alcohol had taken out of him. As for the huge cigars (the older he became, the more often were they gifts from admirers and friends), it was observed that he mumbled and played with them rather than seriously smoked them, and they seem not to have been held responsible for his occasional chest troubles. His most evident recurrent affliction was not physical but psychological: depression. He was familiar enough with it to call it familiarly his 'black dog', a bout of gloom and despair that came over him directly after big disappointments and when he had no challenge to meet. Much has been written about this since it became public knowledge in the book his personal physician Lord Moran published very soon after he died, but its importance has been exaggerated. It never stopped him doing anything he wanted to do.

---

*Figure. 9.2 - Extract from 'Churchill - A Study in Greatness'*
Reproduced with permission and thanks to Prof. Best

## Step 1 - Recap

If you are reading a biography, you have become familiar with the subject matter. So a recap is not necessary.

## Step 2 - Objectives

To do this Chapter full justice, one could have three objectives.

1. What kind of man had Churchill become by 1930?
2. Why is Chartwell important?
3. How did he become aware of the German threat, when others did not?

Since the extract above is limited to a couple of pages and this is an exercise, I limit my objective to the first.

## Step 3 - Overview

Zig-zag through the piece, four lines at a time. It seems that this summarises the main events in Churchill's political life. Then we move on to discovering him physically and psychologically, as if we were observing a friend. Notice that there is little 'bumf' in these descriptions - at least with regards to the objective.

## Step 4 - Preview and Step 5 - Inview

Combine these steps because there is no need to cross anything out. It is the speed of reading that will change: faster over the passages that are less interesting - to me the reader - and slower on those that enlighten me, the reader. Notice here that this selection of speed is highly subjective. It all depends on what you are looking for.

The first paragraph reminds us that Churchill is a family man. The second and third that he is a great man in the making. I read these quickly, and the same for the fourth which sums up his past experience, read also quite quickly.

But now I slow down, as if I were walking with this man and was looking at him more closely. I learn about his character: I had not realised that he exercised! And so we move to his depressions which he dealt with, it seems successfully.

## 6. Review

You may, or may not want to make notes. But if you did, here is an example of a Mind Map®, based on the comments above.

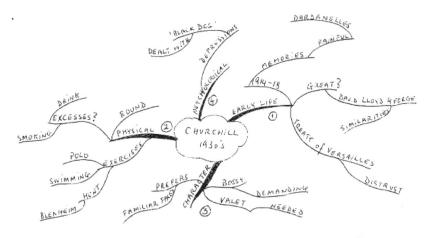

*Figure 9.3 - Mind Map of 'Churchill in the 1930s'*

If you were to continue to read this Chapter of Churchill's life, you would discover that much-loved Chartwell provides the shelter where Churchill did most of his writing and becomes a hub to meet friends and family. As for Germany, Churchill's worry goes back a long way: 1919 and the Treaty of Versailles. But if you wish to know more, you will have to read the book.

# 10

# How to Present and Edit a Document

---

**THE PRESENTATION OF A PAGE**

**TIPS FOR THE EFFECTIVE PRESENTATION OF DOCUMENTS**

**FIRST IMPRESSIONS COUNT**

**FOUR STEPS TO EDIT A DOCUMENT**

---

This chapter examines the presentation of documents. If you wish to be read, make documents attractive to the reader. It also offers a structured approach to editing documents. This last technique is adapted from the six-step approach described in Chapter 8.

## The presentation of a page

Spend five seconds looking at a typical book page, as set out in Figure 10.1.

*Figure 10.1 - An unimaginative book page (overleaf)*

## Personal Development

All successful people have a common denominator: they have firmly established and clearly planned goals which they are moving towards. Only about 3% of people take the time to plan specific aims and objectives. It is therefore hardly surprising that success is not a common occurrence. You should start today on your road to being successful by planning your own future. Procrastination will only delay your goal achievement.

The art of 'Goal Setting' is worth learning and you will benefit from the time spent. Furthermore, by helping your new team members to set both short- and long-term goals you will be able to help them to formulate a sense of purpose and direction in their lives.

Goals need to be clearly written down, showing exactly what you and your colleagues wish to achieve. For instance, a specific amount of sales, or to qualify for promotion. Some goals may relate to being able to purchase household items, or being able to lake a foreign holiday. Whatever the goal may be, it should always be in writing with a realistic time scale set for its achievement. Always remember to encourage your team members to be keen to share their aims and ambitions with you, so that you can help them achieve their goals. You should always target the challenges which must be met, and the action which must be taken to arrive at a chosen goal. This process will help you develop as a leader who is committed to goal achievement.

People react in a positive way to others who know where and why they are going. By setting goals you, in turn, motivate yourself with a sense of purpose. You know exactly where you are going, the vital ingredient for success.

As a motivated leader who wants to achieve success you must continually assess your goals. Sometimes I might be necessary to change direction, but not the goal. Flexibility in reaching your objective is important.

If you try one particular way and fail, do not give up. Look again and see if you can find a different route to success. Be receptive to new ideas and suggestions. There is always an alternative way to overcome a particular challenge. By helping your team members to achieve their goals you will also be reaching some of your goals.

People don't achieve success by luck or chance. When you look closely at successful people you will see a motivated person who is fully aware of where they are going, how long it will take, and what they need to do to get there.

**?** How does it appeal to you? How do you react?
**?** Would you want to read it?
**?** Why?

If your reaction is rather negative, the cause is probably because:

- you had to pay attention to the length of the lines; the more words per line, the more difficult to read
- you have to look for clues leading to important items in the text - the uniformity of presentation makes this search difficult
- the impression is of characterless bulk - the page is too full and lacks interest.

The same page could be presented as shown in Figure 10.2 overleaf.

*Figure 10.2 - A well laid out book page (overleaf)*

## The Art of Goal Setting

Successful people have a common denominator. They are moving towards firmly established and clearly planned goals. Only about 3% of people plan specific aims and objectives for their life. Therefore it is not surprising that success is not a common occurrence in everyday life. You should start today to plan for success by planning your own future. Procrastination will only delay your goal achievement.

The art of 'Goal Setting' is worth learning and you will benefit from the time spent. Also, by helping your new team members to set both short- and long-term goals you will be able to help them to formulate a sense of purpose and direction in their lives.

## How do you set goals?

**Goals need to be written**, showing clearly what you and your colleagues wish to achieve, for example, a specific amount of sales, or to sponsor a set number of people into the business, or to qualify for the company foreign conference. Some goals may relate to being able to purchase household items, or being able to afford a family holiday. Whatever the goal may be, it should always be in writing with a realistic time scale set for its achievement. Always remember to encourage your team members to be keen to share their aims and ambitions with you, so that you can help them achieve their goals. You should always target the challenges which must be met, and the action which must be taken to arrive at a chosen goal. This process will help you develop as a leader who is committed to goal achievement.

## The benefits of goal setting

People react in a positive way to those who know where they are going and why they are going there. By setting goals you, in turn, motivate yourself with a sense of purpose. You know exactly where you are going, the **vital ingredient for success**.

As a *motivated leader* who wants to achieve success you must continually assess your own and colleagues' goals. Sometimes it might be necessary to change direction, but not the goal: flexibility in reaching your objective is important.

If you try one particular way and fail, do not give up. Look again to see if you can find a different route to success. Be receptive to new ideas and suggestions. There is always an alternative way to overcome a particular challenge. By helping your team members to achieve their goals you will also be reaching some of your own goals.

People don't achieve success by luck or chance. When you look closely at successful people you will see motivated people who are fully aware of where they are going, how long it will take, and *what they need to do to get there.*

## Tips for the effective presentation of documents

When you are writing a document, do you ever pause to think about the reader? Indeed, do you want to be read? If you do, remember that what is unattractive to you will, probably, be unattractive to others. Well-presented documents can make the difference between successful sales and failure.

---

### 11 tips for the effective presentation of documents

- Reduce the number of words per line: maximum ten.
- Write, where possible, in double spacing.
- Have a maximum of one idea or subject per paragraph.
- Use different fonts to emphasise particular points in your message.
- In reports and similar documents, put a summary at the front.
- In documents over a few pages long, have an appropriate table of contents.
- Columns are easier to read than wide lines.
- Use appropriate icons to draw the reader's eye to key categories of information.
- Use diagrams, graphics and illustrations in preference to text.
- Introduce different subject sections with clear headings.
- Look at the document and ask yourself 'If I received this document would it invite me to read it?'

---

## First impressions count

How often, when meeting someone for the first time, have you made up your mind about the person in the first five minutes (or even the first ten seconds)? How quickly, as you browse in a bookshop, do you make up your mind about buying a book?

*Exercise:* Where do you hunt for ideas? What people, places, activities, and situations do you use to get new ideas?

I've asked many people this question. Here are some of their ideas.

*Magic.* Through the study and performance of magic, I've learned the power that certain symbols have when they are associated with one another. I've taken this knowledge and applied it to sales and product demonstrations.

*Acting Class.* From acting class I have been able to appreciate the impact that positive encouragement has on a person. I have seen some performances that were so bad I was embarrassed to watch. But the acting coach gave the person criticism in an encouraging way. As a result, these people were able to grow as actors. I think that there is a lesson here for many areas of life.

*Family Trips.* Whenever our family goes on vacation, I have made it a practice to take them on a tour through an operating plant to see how things are made and what procedures are used. We have seen sheet factories, record factories, distilleries, and ceramic factories.

*Junk Yards.* Going to a junk yard is a sobering experience/There you can see the ultimate destination of almost everything we desire.

*Different People.* I like to spend time with people whose value systems are different from my own. I like to see what's important to them, and that gives me a perspective on what's important to me.

*Figure 10.3 - First Impressions Count*

First impressions count. By how much? The example in Figure 10.3 is taken from Roger von Oech's clever and witty book on creativity, *A Whack on the Side of the Head* (4), which demonstrates concern for the reader.

# Four steps to edit a document

> ### *Case Study*
>
> Consider now the case of Sandra, a surveyor in a large retail organisation. Sandra has requested three independent architects (A, B and C) to tender for the design of a supermarket which is to be built. By the tender closing date, each architect has responded, and Sandra examines the tenders.
>
> Architect A's tender is attractively and clearly presented Sandra quiokly finds the key items she is looking for - a summary at the front, previous experience of this type of work, and costs. The architect has written the tender with Sandra in mind and has clearly labelled each section of the bid.
>
> The two other tenders (B and C) are poorly arranged and it is difficult to locate information; the print is small and there is too much information per page. Without clear headings, Sandra will have to dig for the information she wants the hard way. If you were Sandra, what would your thoughts be now?
>
> - A favourable impression which increases the chances of success for Architect A?
> - A supplier who has you in mind when tendering for a job will tend to keep your needs in mind if the job becomes theirs?
> - Conversely Architects B and C do not seem to care about Sandra's current requirements. Will they care in the future?

All documents are written to sell something. (Otherwise what is the point of writing?) If you were to build a new house, where would you start? Would you first establish the kind of taps you wanted for the bathroom? Probably not. You might start with drawing an outline picture of the whole house and garage. The picture will have some key features. Either it will show a porch with pillars, or a long bungalow or large top-to-bottom windows - whatever you want. Then you might think of the materials you want to use - stone, brick, wood, slate or thatch, and insulation.

Once your house is designed, you turn your attention to fitting it out - what type of bathroom taps and kitchen sink - and when it is built, to decorating it. In other words you concentrate on the structure before getting down to the details.

Editing a document requires a similar approach or frame of mind. To edit a document, apply a similar approach to the six steps described in Chapter 8. But here you need only four steps as shown in Figure 10.4

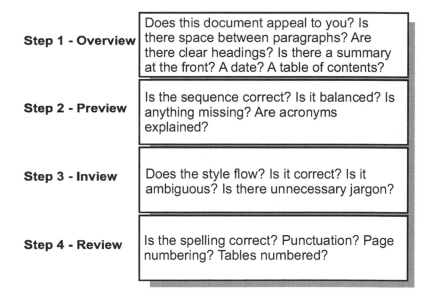

| Step 1 - Overview | Does this document appeal to you? Is there space between paragraphs? Are there clear headings? Is there a summary at the front? A date? A table of contents? |
| Step 2 - Preview | Is the sequence correct? Is it balanced? Is anything missing? Are acronyms explained? |
| Step 3 - Inview | Does the style flow? Is it correct? Is it ambiguous? Is there unnecessary jargon? |
| Step 4 - Review | Is the spelling correct? Punctuation? Page numbering? Tables numbered? |

*Figure 10.4 - Four steps to edit a document*

## Step I

Flick through the whole document to gain a general impression, as you would do in a bookshop. It is useful here to unstaple the document and lay it flat, sequentially page by page on a long table, or the floor if you do not have a table surface long enough. The idea is to get a general impression holistically.

● *If you are unhappy with what you see, send the document back to the author with your comments. She or he will need to correct the presentation before you examine the document more closely.*

## Step 2

Take a closer look, skimming about four lines at a time to gauge the sequence and the balance. If the document is to compare x, y and z, does it give equal space to each or space in proportion to the importance of each?

● *If you wish to change the sequence, for example, put paragraph seven ahead of paragraph three, send the document to the author with your comment before reading it carefully as in step three.*

## Step 3

Read carefully the whole document at your own speed (cruising speed); you are checking for style, that statements are factually correct, and that the document sets out its statements clearly and in a logical order. Try to delay correcting spelling and other small details until later.

● *If you have many comments to make, send the document back to the author before proceeding to step four.*

## Step 4

Check all the typographical details.

### The benefits of the four-step approach

- At each step, both editor and writer know where they stand and are less likely to make mistakes or invest a lot of work which is wasted by subsequent alterations.

- Each step meets a clear objective. The approach starts with a broad view and progressively moves towards the more detailed work.

- The editor's job is to ensure that the document is assembled in the most effective manner and proceeds logically towards its goal. He or she does this by comment and suggestion. The writer's job is to set down the facts (or fiction), following the editor's guidance, and to look after the details to produce a polished work. Editing a document does not mean rewriting it for a poor author. Editing can, therefore, teach a writer how to write better in future.

For a really detailed and inspiring book about writing reports, see *The Report Report* by Alasdair Drysdale (23)

# Bumf-free Future ...

I hope that the experiences, exercises and tips have given you, the reader, some ideas on the question of bumf. But you will not have an automatic improvement in your bumf-handling ability unless you DO most of the exercises described here. Only a few minutes a day practice will soon turn you into an effective bumf disposer and an discriminating information gatherer. Anything that you can do to streamline the amount of bumf that surrounds you is a step in the right direction.

The computer has entered our offices and homes and with it, more bumf problems. But the computer does bring one skill that no one person possesses, the ability to scan enormous numbers of records according to any selection instructions which have been fed into it. Some manufacturers have designed software that, in addition to recording minutes of meetings and notes about telephone conversations, will also pass on the information to the right people at the right time. If ever you are faced with the task of organising a large quantity of information, which much current legislation requires to be kept, a computer will help you, but it cannot yet prune out the bumf unless you tell it to. Good luck!

# Bibliography

The following books are either referenced in the text ( ) or are recommended for further reading to provide you with new insights to stimulate your creativity in business affairs.

1. John Holt, *How Children Learn*, Penguin, 1967
2. Douglas R.Hofstadter, *Metamagical Themas: Questing for the Essence of Mind and Pattern,* Penguin, 1985
3. Frank Smith, *Reading*, Cambridge University Press, 1978
4. Roger von Oech, *A Whack on the Side of the Head*, Warner Books, N.Y., 1983
5. Shoshana Zuboff, *The Age of the Smart Machine*, Heinemann Professional Publishing, 1988
6. Alan McAuslan, *Dyslexia: What Parents Ought to Know*, Penguin, London
7. Anthony Smith, *The Mind*, Viking, London, 1984
8. The British Dyslexia Association, Church Lane, Peppard, Oxfordshire RG9 5JN
9. Kathryn Redway, *How to be a Rapid Reader*, National Textbook Company, Lincolnwood, Ill. USA, 1991
10. W. H. Bates, *Better Eyesight Without Glasses*, Grafton, 1979
11. A. R. Luria, *The Working Brain*, Penguin, London
12. J. Z. Young, *Programs of the Brain*, OUP, Oxford, 1978
13. Gary Small M.D., *The Memory Prescription*, Hyperion Books, 2004
14. Tony Buzan, *Use Your Head*, BBC Publications, London, 1982
15. Direct Mail information Service, The Letterbox File, 1993
16. A. V. Akro, B. W. Kemighan and P. W. Weinberger, *The AWK Programming Language,* Addison-Wesley, 1988
17. R. S. Wurman, *Information Anxiety*, Pan Books 1991
18. G. Nadler and S. Hibino, *Breakthrough Thinking*, Prima Publishing, 1990
19. Tony Buzan, *The Mind Map® Book,* BBC Publications, 1995

20. Mark H. McCormack, *What They Don't Teach You at Harvard Business School*, Bantam Books, 1985
21. John B. Arden, *Improving Your Memory for Dummies*, Wiley Publishing, 2002
22. Professor Geoffrey Best, *'Churchill - a Study in Greatness'*, Hambledon and London, 2001
23. Alasdair Drysdale, *The Report Report*, Management Books 2000 Ltd, Kemble, 2004

# Index